P9-DOH-109

CONTENTS

To those who find that the more they look,
the more they know.

WILDFLOWERS
of the
EAST

Written and Illustrated by
MABEL CRITTENDEN
and
DOROTHY TELFER

Celestial Arts
Millbrae, California

cover photo: Mary Ferguson
color separation for cover: Herzig Somerville Limited, Toronto,
    Canada
cover design: Betsy Bruno

Copyright © 1977 by Mabel Crittenden and Dorothy Telfer

Celestial Arts
231 Adrian Road
Millbrae, California 94030

No part of this book may be reproduced by any mechanical,
photographic, or electronic process, or in the form of a
phonographic recording, nor may it be stored in a retrieval
system, transmitted, or otherwise be copied for public or private
use without the written permission of the publisher.

First Printing, August, 1977

Made in the United States of America

Library of Congress Cataloging in Publication Data

Crittenden, Mabel, 1917-
    Wildflowers of the East.

    Bibliography: p.
    Includes index.
    1. Wild flowers—United States—Identification.
I. Telfer, Dorothy W., joint author. II. Title.
QK115.C74   582'.13'0974   77-79878
ISBN 0-89087-132-9

1 2 3 4 5 6 7 8 – 82 81 80 79 78 77

PREFACE

There has long been a need for a book such as this. So many people look at wildflowers and wish they really knew something more about them—and more than just their names.

The fascinating fact about wildflowers, or anything else—particularly in nature—is that the more you know about them and look closely at them, the more you really see. And this book leads a person to just that, for to use this book, you must really LOOK at a flower, its parts, (including edibility—indicated by a 😋 , 😖 in the margin) how it is put together, how and where it grows—and as you study it, you really begin to see.

Early generations of Americans enjoyed fields and forests filled with acres of lovely wildflowers. Today most such lands have been plowed or paved over. Only in woodlots, meadows, parks, and wilderness areas are such lands being preserved. Fortunately, many people are becoming increasingly concerned with saving some of this loveliness so future generations will not be denied this way of refreshing their spirits.

It is our hope that this book will enhance your enjoyment of wildflowers and that then you, too, will help preserve them for everybody.

—the Authors

Chapter I

CLUES TO FLOWER IDENTIFICATION

Flower Parts

1. *SEPALS* The outermost circle of parts are the *sepals*. While the flower is in the bud stage, the sepals are wrapped around all the other parts to protect them. In a few flowers, the sepals are pushed off when the bud opens. In others, they turn downward under the open petals. In some, they stay on and surround the growing ovary. In a few flowers, the sepals remain on the plant long after the petals drop and the seeds are scattered.

In most flowers, the sepals are green, but they may be brightly colored and look so much like petals that it may be easy to confuse them. This is true of many Lilies and Irises. Although the petals and sepals may be colored alike, they are arranged in two circles. The outer ones are the sepals, the inner ones the petals. Thus, Lilies have three sepals and three petals, not six petals, as they seem to have.

If the flower has only one circle of petal-like parts, botanists speak of them as sepals, even if they are brightly colored and look like petals. All the sepals together are called the *calyx*. This term is used most frequently when the sepals are united. Count the tips to determine the number of fused sepals.

2. *PETALS*   Inside the sepals are the *petals*, the color-ful, attractive part of the flower. All petals together are the *corolla*, sometimes united into a *corolla tube*. Count the petal lobes to know the number of fused petals. Petals vary in shape and number in different types of flowers. They may be all alike or an irregular vase-shaped corolla with upper and lower lips, like a snapdragon. The petals usually fade and drop after the seeds begin to develop. A few flow-ers have no petals. The number of petals and whether or not they are united is so basic that the chapters of this book are arranged on that basis.

3. *STAMENS*   The *stamens* form the third circle. Often they are the yellow, fuzzy part in the flower center, but they may be any color and vary in number, depending on the flower group. A few flowers have no stamens. The stamens are the male organs which produce the pollen used to fertilize the ovules of the flower. Pollen is a powder made up of very tiny grains, or spores, which comes out of the little bag, or sac, at the tip of the stamen called the *anther*, held at the end of a slender stalk called the *filament*. Some-times the filaments are united in a collar around the *pistil*.

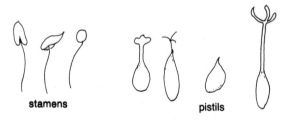

stamens   pistils

4. *PISTIL*   The *pistil* is the female organ, the seed-producing part of the flower. It is made up of three parts: (1) the top is the *stigma* which catches the pollen; it may open into furry or sticky branches when it is mature. (2) the *style* connects the stigma to the third part of the pistil, and holds the stigma at the right height to fit the needs of that flower; not every flower has a style. (3) the *ovary* is the enlarged

base of the pistil; it is a bag holding the *ovules* which are the future seeds. A *superior ovary* is up inside the blossom, with petals, sepals, and stamens attached below it. If the ovary is below where the petals are attached, it is called an *inferior ovary*. Usually you can see the inferior ovary by looking at the back or underside of the flower. To see a superior ovary, you must look into the flower. This is especially true if the petals or sepals are united.

After the ovules are fertilized, they develop into seeds. As the seeds grow, the ovary grows larger and develops the *fruit*, which is the mature ovary, containing mature seeds. A flower may have one, two, or many pistils, which may be simple with one ovule, or compound, made of many united sections and developing several ovules. The number of pistils generally matches the number of petals.

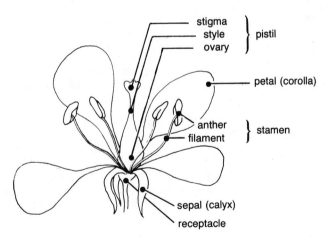

Other Clues to Help Identify Flowers

1. The *receptacle* is the enlarged end of the flower stem in which the flower sits. It usually appears to be a continuation of the stem.

2. *Bracts* are not found on all flowers. They are specialized leaves which may look like sepals or petals. They often are brightly colored, but they enclose a *group* of flowers—sepals enclose just one flower. The red "petals"

bract holding 3 flowers

of poinsetta are bracts. The individual flowers of these plants are very tiny and not easily noticed, but they contain the necessary parts, the pistils and stamens, and so are the true flowers of the plant.

3. *Specialized Arrangements*   In the huge Sunflower or Composite Family, the blossoms are made up of *many* tiny flowers, surrounded by bracts. These modified leaves form an involucre around the tightly clustered flowers. It is as though someone had taken a stem of flowers and pushed them all up to the top into a tight head, surrounded by some of the leaves which also were pushed up. In flowers like daisies and sunflowers, the center might *seem* to be the stamens. Look closely and see that these are tiny flowers all packed together, each having petals, stamens and pistil. Pull a head carefully apart. These center flowers are called *disc flowers*. Each has a corolla of five tiny petals, united

BRACTS FORMING AN INVOLUCRE HOLDING
MANY SEPARATE FLOWERS

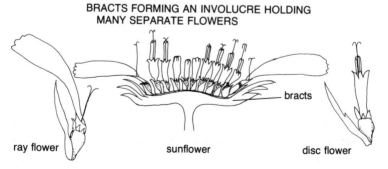

bracts

ray flower   sunflower   disc flower

into a tiny tube, with just the tips free. There are five stamens held in tightly by the petals. The simple pistil has an inferior ovary, with a slender style, and a stigma which opens into two branches to catch the pollen. The calyx is very reduced and in many plants of this family is merely made of hairs or fuzz like the dandelion fuzz which is seen in the fluffy seed head.

In daisies, the disc flowers are surrounded by "petals"; really they are tiny modified one-sided flowers. These are called *ray* flowers, and have been developed to advertise the disc flowers so all will be pollinated by insects. These ray flowers may have just stamens or just pistils or neither, and some show three to five petal lobes separated by notches at the tips.

Flowers may be arranged several ways: *solitary*, with just one blossom at the end of a branch (as Poppy); an *umbel*, with many small flowers grouped together at the same height (Wild Carrot), and more or less flat across the top; a *head* with many flowers growing together in a rounded arrangement; a *spike* and a *raceme* have several flowers growing along the branch. A *spadix* is a thick-stemmed spike, the flowers usually without petals, and is enclosed by a *spathe*.

SPECIALIZED ARRANGEMENTS

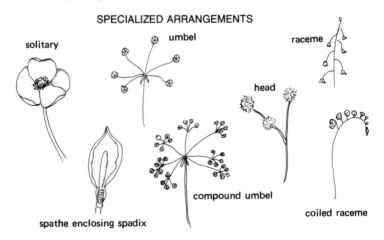

solitary

umbel

raceme

head

compound umbel

spathe enclosing spadix

coiled raceme

4. *Habitat* is the kind of home in which the flower grows best, such as woods or sunny fields, etc. This may be still another clue to identification. In describing each flower, we have given its habitat.

5. *Kind of fruit* is often a clue to identification. A fruit is anything that holds the ripened seeds of the plants—not just something we eat. Often the fruits of wildflowers can scarcely be seen covering the ripe seeds. The fruit is formed from the ovary, sometimeswith other parts included, as the receptacle in apples and berries. Some fruits are berries, some are dry capsules or pods. Some have a single hard

KINDS OF FRUIT

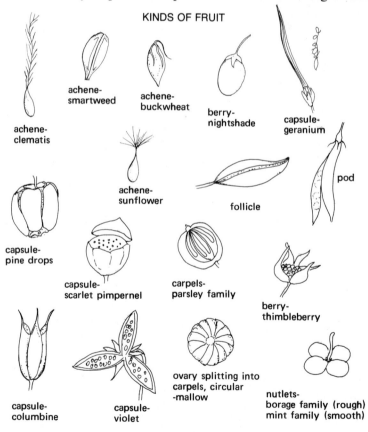

achene-
smartweed

achene-
buckwheat

berry-
nightshade

capsule-
geranium

achene-
clematis

achene-
sunflower

follicle

pod

capsule-
pine drops

capsule-
scarlet pimpernel

carpels-
parsley family

berry-
thimbleberry

capsule-
columbine

capsule-
violet

ovary splitting into
carpels, circular
-mallow

nutlets-
borage family (rough)
mint family (smooth)

seed, like plums; some are small and hard with one seed inside, like a sunflower. Some, like dandelion and thistle, have silky "parachutes" to carry them; some have burrs or hooks to help them get carried. Every ovary will mature into fruit if even one of its ovules is fertilized; the ovule develops into a seed and the ovary becomes the fruit, or container of the seed.

6. *Leaves* may help distinguish flower families or similar flowers from each other. The expanded part of the leaf is called the *blade*; the *petiole* is the stalk which attaches it to the plant. Usually leaves in which the blade is long and narrow have veins that run parallel to the leaf edge. These are called *parallel-veined* leaves, and are typical of Lily, Iris and Grass Families. If the veins form a network in the blade, we call the leaf *netted-veined*. Most plants have this type of veins.

The blade of netted-veined leaves may be many shapes: broad, round, oval, heart-shaped, etc. The margin of the blade may be smooth, toothed, notched, lobed, etc. It may be deeply divided (as in Squirrel Corn or Dutchman's Breeches leaves). There are two ways veins can be arranged: *pinnately* (as a feather) with side veins branching all along the main vein; *palmately* with several veins radiating from one point (as fingers from the palm of your hand). Deeply lobed leaves are often palmately veined.

Leaves are *simple* when there is only one blade. The leaf is called *compound* when the blade is divided clear to the midrib, making several leaflets on the same petiole. There are two kinds of compound leaves: *pinnately compound*, when leaflets are arranged along the length of the petiole (roses); *palmately compound,* when leaflets are arranged radiating from the end of the petiole (lupine, clover).

The way leaves are arranged on the plant is often a clue to identification. On some plants the leaves grow directly from the crown of the roots, around the base of the flower stalk (as in most Evening Primroses). These are called

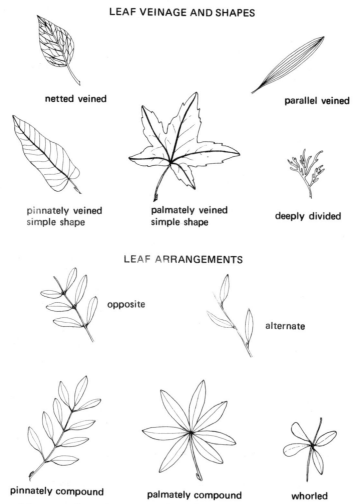

LEAF VEINAGE AND SHAPES

netted veined

parallel veined

pinnately veined
simple shape

palmately veined
simple shape

deeply divided

LEAF ARRANGEMENTS

opposite

alternate

pinnately compound

palmately compound

whorled

basal leaves, forming a *rosette*. On most plants, the leaves grow along the branches. If only one leaf grows at a place with leaves alternating up the branch, they are called *alternate*. If two grow at one place, one on each side of the branch, they are called *opposite*. If several grow at one place, all around the stem, they are called *whorled*. If the leaves seem to sit right on the stem, they are called *sessile*.

Chapter II

FOLLOWING THE CLUES

Follow the Clues of the petal numbers

Notice the printed tabs that appear on the right side of the following pages. These tabs represent petals and give clues for finding your flowers with their descriptions and pictures. Flowers with three petals are described and pictured on pages with three printed tabs. If your flower has four petals, look on the pages with four printed tabs on the margin. If the petals grow together at the base (fused to the next one), the printed tabs are united, so look on those pages. If the printed tabs are not all the same size, then flowers whose petals are not all the same size or shape will be found on those pages. There you will find pictures to match your flower, and many interesting facts about it. So, count your petals and look for the same number of tabs.

OR

Follow the Clues of the Botanical Key

Carefully inspect your flower. Find the petals and sepals. Count them. Are they united or separate? How many stamens and pistils are there? Where is the ovary located? Look at both buds and open flowers to find all parts; look at more than one flower. Look at the leaves.

NOW: Look at the KEY that begins on page 11. The clues are in words and pictures and are arranged in pairs or triplets. Your flower will fit one of the first set. Does it fit clue 1a or 1b? When you decide, follow the direction the clue gives you.

Let's use the KEY to identify Spring Beauty. How many petals, sepals, stamens, and pistils does it have? Are any of them united? It has five petals, two sepals, five stamens, and one pistil with three styles.

Look at the KEY. Notice the illustrations with each clue—they help you decide. In clue 1 you decide if the plant is aquatic or not. Spring Beauty is not aquatic, so it fits 1b, not 1a. Do as the KEY says—go to clue 2. There are three choices here: read all three and decide which fits. It is not like a daisy, thistle, or dandelion, so it does not fit clue 2a; it is not a tiny flower on a spadix (see illustration for what a spadix looks like), so it does not fit 2b, but it does fit 2c. This tells us to go to clue 3. Clue 3a fits flowers with no petals or sepals; our flower has both, so 3b sends us to clue 4. Clue 4a is for flowers with parts in threes—doesn't fit; clue 4b is for flowers in fours or fives, so that does fit; but check what 4c says: "more than five petals"—so only 4b is right and sends us to clue 8. Clue 8a says "has sepals but no petals"—no, clue 8b has both petals and sepals—yes, go to clue 10. Clue 10a, flower parts separate—yes, for each petal can be pulled off without tearing the next one; on to clue 11. Which clue is right here? Clue 11b is, for there are ten or fewer stamens (five), which sends us to clue 17. The ovary is superior (see illustration), for it is above where the petals and sepals are attached, so our flower fits 17a, which sends us to clue 18. The petals are all the same shape (18b), so on to 20. There are five petals (20b), so go to clue 21. The leaves are not palmately compound (21b), so on to clue 22. And, 22a fits our flower! It is in the Purslane Family. Turn to page 112 where the family characteristics are given, with illustrations and descriptions of common members of that family.

After you have practiced using the KEY a few times, you will become expert with it and be able to find the family of the common eastern wildflowers. However, you *must* remember the circles, so you can distinguish between petals and sepals, and when keying flowers in heads, you *must* be sure to take the head apart so you are looking at *only one flower*. This is especially true of the Composite Family which has many tiny flowers tightly grouped together and surrounded by leafy bracts. They seem to have many *petals*; really they have many *flowers*.

Not all flowers you find will necessarily be in this book; we have tried to put the most common ones here, in forty-five different families. Even if the flower you find is not here, you probably can find what family it is in, then go to another book and perhaps find it there—especially if you then use one of the large-sized, restricted regional books.

Count the petals and have fun!

The Key

Carefully examine one flower. Count the sepals, petals, stamens, and pistils. Open a flower or cut it in half if you need to. Count lobes for the number of petals if they are united. Notice if the plant is growing in water.

1 a. Aquatic plants growing in water with leaves in, on, or standing above water; leaves generally large . . .   turn to page 206

a.    b.

b. Not aquatic plants growing in water—may grow on banks or in edges of marshes . . .   go to clue 2

2 a. Flowers are numerous and tiny in a compact head surrounded by a green involucre of many sepal-like bracts; flowers daisy-like, thistle-like or dandelion-like—the Composite Family . . .

turn to page 181

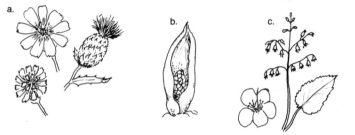

b. Flowers are numerous and tiny, on a spadix surrounded by a spathe— the Arum Family . . .

turn to page 42

c. Flowers not in compact head or on a spadix (flowers may be tiny) . . .

go to clue 3

3 a. No petals or sepals; tiny pistillate or staminate flowers subtended by pairs of bracts. Three styles, milky juice—Cypress Spurge . . .

turn to page 46

b. Has both sepals and petals, or only sepals . . .

go to clue 4

4 a. Flower parts are in threes (there may seem to be six, but never four or five); all leaves parallel-veined or grass-like (except Trillium). Wild Lily-of-the-Valley has parts in twos, (see page 52), also see Impatience (page 74) . . .   go to clue 5

b. Flower parts are in fours or fives but not in threes; leaves netted-veined. (see also Impatience, page 74) . . .   go to clue 8

c. Each flower has sepals, and more than five true petals . . .   turn to page 175

5 a. Ovary is superior (above attachment of calyx and corolla—you may have to open flower) . . .   go to clue 6

b. The ovary is inferior (below base of petals) . . .   go to clue 7

6 a. Stems jointed; 3 green persistent sepals, 3 quickly-withering fragile petals (lowest petal may be smaller), usually blue—the Spiderwort Family . . .

turn to page 72

 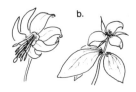

b. Stems not jointed; 3 sepals and 3 petals colored and shaped more or less alike; or 3 green sepals and 3 withering-persistent petals (with netted veins)—the Lily Family . . .

turn to page 48

7 a. Inferior ovary with Lily-like flowers usually in umbels; lower part of petals and sepals may be united; 6 stamens (or 3 stamens and 3 staminoidea)—the Amaryllis Family . . .

turn to page 60

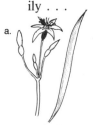 

b. Inferior ovary, only 3 stamens; 3-parted stigma may be petal-like; sheathing leaves—the Iris Family . . .

turn to page 62

c. Inferior ovary, lowest petal different—may be larger, saccate, lipped, different color; lower sepals may be fused so there seems to be only two; stamen and style united, forming a central column—the Orchid Family . . .

turn to page 65

8   a. Flowers have sepals but no petals (calyx may be colored and appear petal-like, but there will be only one circle of "petals," not two as when you have *both* petals and sepals) . . .   go to clue 9

b. Flowers have *both* sepals and petals (some flowers lose sepals early, so look at both buds and flowers) . . .   go to clue 10

9   a. Calyx of 5 or 6 parts, pinkish, reddish, yellowish, greenish, or whitish, drying persistent; single superior ovary; 4-12 stamens—the Buckwheat Family . . .   turn to page 29

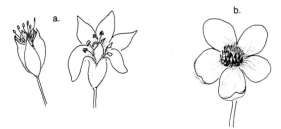

b. Calyx of 4 or 5 parts, often petal-like or colored; calyx may fall early; surrounds *many* 1-celled, simple pistils clustered on a mound; many stamens—the Buttercup Family . . .   turn to page 85

10 a. Petals are separate from each other, not joined (lower 2 petals in pea-shaped flowers seem lightly joined and shaped like a canoe) . . .   go to clue 11

      b. Petals are joined to each other, at least at base . . .   go to clue 28

11 a. More than 10 stamens (more than double number of petals) . . .   go to clue 12

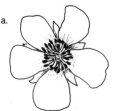

      b. 10 stamens or less . . .   go to clue 17

12 a. Plants with pitcher-shaped or trumpet-shaped basal leaves; nodding flower on leafless stem—the Pitcher Plant Family . . .   turn to page 108

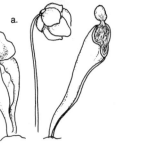
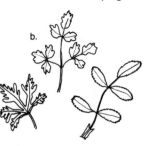

      b. Plants do not have pitcher-shaped or trumpet-shaped leaves . . .   go to clue 13

13 a. Stamens united by filaments into tube surrounding pistil—the Mallow Family . . .

turn to page 104

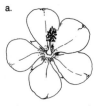

b. Stamens not united by filaments into tube . . .

go to clue 14

14 a. Two or more ovaries clustered together but each separate; may be grouped atop a small central mound or partly or completely enclosed by calyx tube . . .

go to clue 15

b. One ovary, may be compound with one to many styles or stigmas (Saxifrage ovaries may be only lightly joined) . . .

go to clue 16

15 a. Sepals separate; numerous stamens attached to receptacle below petals and pistils (not attached to sepals); simple separate superior ovaries on small central mound (if corolla is irregular see Larkspur pg 85)— Buttercup Family . . .   turn to page 85

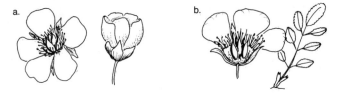

b. Sepals united at base, numerous stamens attached to the calyx or to a disc or rim that lines calyx cup. Tiny pair of leaflike structures (stipules) at base of leaves; leaves usually compound—the Rose Family . . .   turn to page 95

16 a. Calyx falls as corolla opens; stamens attached to base of petals but not to each other—the Poppy Family . . .   turn to page 176

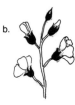

b. Calyx remaining after corolla opens; stamens united or not . . .   go to clue 17

17 a. Superior ovary . . .   go to clue 18

b. Inferior ovary . . .   go to clue 27

18
a. Petals *not* all the same shape— corolla irregular . . .

go to clue 19

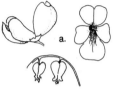

b. Petals all the same shape (or almost) . . .

go to clue 20

19
a. Corolla somewhat like that of sweet peas (one large upper petal which may be folded over others, 2 side petals, and 2 stuck-together lower petals shaped like a canoe— the Pea Family . . .

turn to page 125

b. Corolla like Pansies or Violets (2 upright petals, 2 side petals, 1 lower petal with a spur)—the Violet Family . . .

turn to page 130

c. 4 petals of two unlike, overlapping pairs; 2 scale-like sepals; 2 groups of 3 stamens—the Fumitory Family . . .

turn to page 87

20
a. 4 petals, 4 sepals, 6 stamens (4 of them tall, 2 short)—the Mustard Family . . .

turn to page 77

b. 5 petals . . .

go to clue 21

21 a. Leaves palmately compound, resembling clover—the Oxalis Family . . .

turn to page 110

b. Leaves not palmately compound . . .

go to clue 22

22 a. 2 sepals (usually), 5 stamens (usually), 3 styles (usually), flowers wither quickly—the Purslane Family . . .

turn to page 112

b. 4 or 5 sepals, sometimes joined into a tube . . .

go to clue 23

23 a. One single persistent style—the Heath Family . . .

turn to page 122

b. 2-5 separate styles, or joined except at tip, tip spreading into 2-5 stigmas . . .

go to clue 24

24 a. 5 styles (closely joined together) with 5 late-opening stigmas; styles grow into long "beaks" as the compound pistil matures, then splits, each style coiling separately with a seed; 10 (sometimes 5) stamens; usually pink or lavender flowers—the Geranium Family . . .

turn to page 99

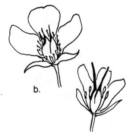

b. 2-5 styles which do not form long "beaks" and remain attached to ovary . . .

go to clue 25

25 a. Basal leaves mostly, or alternate—the Saxifrage Family . . .

turn to page 114

b. Opposite leaves . . .

go to clue 26

26 a. Many stamens, often in 2 or 3 groups at base; 1-3 celled ovary with 3 styles. Leaves and branches

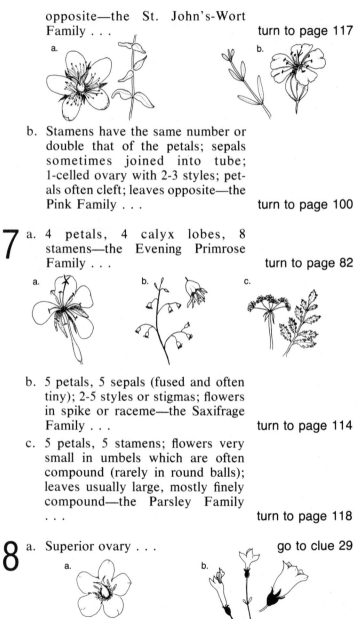

    opposite—the St. John's-Wort
Family . . . turn to page 117

  b. Stamens have the same number or
     double that of the petals; sepals
     sometimes joined into tube;
     1-celled ovary with 2-3 styles; pet-
     als often cleft; leaves opposite—the
     Pink Family . . . turn to page 100

27 a. 4 petals, 4 calyx lobes, 8
     stamens—the Evening Primrose
     Family . . . turn to page 82

  b. 5 petals, 5 sepals (fused and often
     tiny); 2-5 styles or stigmas; flowers
     in spike or raceme—the Saxifrage
     Family . . . turn to page 114

  c. 5 petals, 5 stamens; flowers very
     small in umbels which are often
     compound (rarely in round balls);
     leaves usually large, mostly finely
     compound—the Parsley Family
     . . . turn to page 118

28 a. Superior ovary . . . go to clue 29

  b. Inferior ovary . . . go to clue 38

29

a. Corolla lobes all alike . . .   go to clue 30

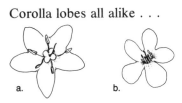

a.   b.   c.

b. Corolla lobes almost alike; tall woolly plants—*Verbascum* in Figwort Family . . .   turn to page 158

c. Corolla appears 2-lipped, or at least not all lobes shaped alike . . .   go to clue 42

30

a. 5-parted cup or "crown" in center with calyx lobes and corolla lobes turned back; milky juice—the Milkweed Family . . .   turn to page 154

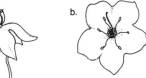

a.   b.   c.

b. No 5-parted cup or "crown" in center; no milky juice; calyx lobes and corolla turned back or not . . .   go to clue 31

31

a. Stamens stand in front of each lobe of corolla; stamens same number as corolla lobes; one style—the Primrose Family . . .   turn to page 142

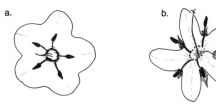

a.   b.

b. Each of the stamens alternate with lobes of the corolla; stamens same number or fewer than lobes . . .   go to clue 32

32 a. Ovary rough and distinctly 4-lobed on outside; one style; flowers in coils which unroll as flowers open—the Borage Family . . .   turn to page 149

a.    b.

b. Ovary compound, but not 4-lobed on outside . . .   go to clue 33

33 a. Flowers large and funnel-shaped (like Morning Glories) . . .   go to clue 34

a. b.

b. Flowers small (unlike Morning Glories) . . .   go to clue 35

34 a. 1 style, 2 stigmas, petals twist in bud, sepals not joined, usually twining—the Morning Glory Family . . .   turn to page 137

a.    b.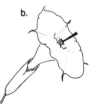

b. 1 style, 1 stigma (2-lobed), sepals, joined into a tube—*Datura* in Nightshade Family . . .   turn to page 152

35 a. Style with 3 stigmas (examine several flowers to be sure stigmas are mature enough to open); 3-celled ovary; 5 petals, 5 sepals, 5 stamens (may be long or short)—the Gilia or Phlox Family . . .   turn to page 144

b. Style not 3-parted; 1- or 2-celled ovary . . .   go to clue 36

36 a. 5 separate (or almost separate) sepals; 2 styles (or 2 stigmas); long stamens; flowers may be in coils which unroll as flowers open—the Phacelia Family . . .   turn to page 147

b. Sepals completely joined except at tip; 1 style . . .   go to clue 37

37 a. 5-lobed corolla with very shallow lobes; leaves alternate; 1 style with 1 stigma—the Nightshade Family . . .   turn to page 152

b. Four- or 5-lobed corolla; leaves opposite; 1-celled ovary—the Gentian Family . . .   turn to page 140

38 a. Flowers separate, not in tight heads . . . go to clue 39

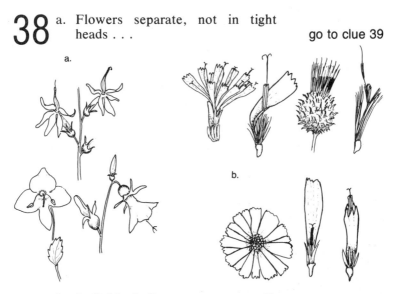

b. Individual flowers very small, tightly gathered into heads held by calyx-like cup of bracts (involucre); flower heads look like daisies, thistles, or dandelions—the Composite Family . . . turn to page 181

39 a. Corolla lobes not alike . . . go to clue 40

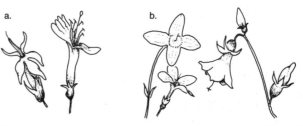

b. Corolla lobes alike . . . go to clue 41

40 a. Corolla 2-lipped, upper lip deeply split; stamens joined around style and protruding through split; leaves alternate—Lobelia, subfamily of Bluebell Family . . . turn to page 156

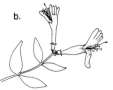

b. Corolla 2-lipped; 5 long stamens; leaves opposite; vines—Honeysuckle Family . . .   turn to page 172

41 a. Corolla bell-shaped with 5 lobes; leaves alternate—Bluebell Family . . .   turn to page 156

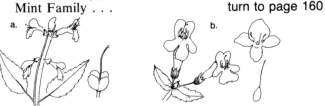

b. Corolla of 4 lobes; leaves opposite or whorled—Madder Family . . .   turn to page 91

42 a. Two-lipped corolla (5 unequal lobes); ovary 4-lobed on outside; stem square (usually); 2 or 4 stamens; opposite leaves with mint odor (usually); often hairy—the Mint Family . . .   turn to page 160

b. Two-lipped corolla of 5 unequal lobes (Veronica has only 4); ovary not 4-lobed: stem not square (except Square-stemmed Monkey Flower); usually 4 stamens with anthers or only 2 with anthers (fifth stamen with no anther in all Penstemon); stamens stand in pairs; often large colorful flowers—the Figwort Family . . .   turn to page 167

Chapter III

FLOWERS WITH SEPALS BUT NO PETALS

Strange as it may seem, some flowers have no petals at all. In many of these flowers the sepals look like the petals; sometimes they are even colored like petals. Or they may look like sepals and the flowers are relatively inconspicuous, like the Sorrels and Smartweeds. In using this book to identify flowers, it is important to examine flowers carefully to make sure whether there are petals and sepals, or just sepals. If there is only one "circle," they are sepals even if they look like petals.

BUCKWHEAT FAMILY
Polygonaceae

The Buckwheat Family has many members growing in all parts of the country—from sea level to high mountains. In the east there are dozens of the genus *Polygonum* (Smartweeds and Knotweeds), while in the west the genus *Eriogonum* is the abundant one. They all have tiny flowers without petals, but the plants often are quite noticeable because there may be so many flowers in spikes, heads, racemes, umbels, etc. Though there are no petals, the blossoms can be quite colorful, the sepals being pink, white, yellow, greenish or brownish and often drying to reds or browns and making excellent dried flowers.

The persistent calyx is usually divided into five or six parts, the stamen number varies from four to twelve, and they are partly attached to the calyx. The one-celled superior ovary with two or three styles produces an achene, often winged. The stems have swollen joints, often with a stipule or leaflet above the joint. The Smartweeds and Knotweeds also have a sheath, with or without a fringe around the swollen joint. Both the Smartweeds and the Knotweeds have pinkish or whitish flowers, the Knotweeds with one or a few in leaf axils and the Smartweeds with tight spikes. Other common "weeds" such as Dock and Sheep Sorrel belong to this family, too.

The alternate leaves are smooth-margined and many species produce a basal cluster. The stem leaves are much smaller. The Buckwheats produce much nectar and so are important plants for honeybees. Buckwheat (for flour) and rhubarb are family members.

Swamp Smartweed, *Polygonum coccineum,* might be included in our water plants chapter for it has a form that is aquatic, but it is also an abundant land plant. The calyx is deep pink and forms long clusters of spikes, much longer than 3 cm (1 in). Otherwise it is very like the Water Smartweed (*P. amphibium*) which, as its name suggests, also has both an aquatic form (not hairy) and a land form (quite hairy). The tight spike is less than

SWAMP SMARTWEED

2.5 cm long. In both (as typical of this genus) the stem is swollen and has a sheath at each leaf joint. Leaves lanceolate, 5-20 cm long (2-8 in), growing in swampy areas and marshlands, abundantly.

Lady's-Thumb, Redleg, *Polygonum persicaria*, is an abundant weed from Europe. The calyx is a pink to purplish color, the flowers forming a tight spike 2-3 cm long (1 in). The papery sheath above each swollen leaf node is fringed. The leaves are nearly sessile, quite narrow, and are 5-15 cm long (2-6 in). The plant is most easily recognized because of a triangular or crescent-shaped dark area about midway on the leaf. The stems may sprawl or grow upright and are reddish.

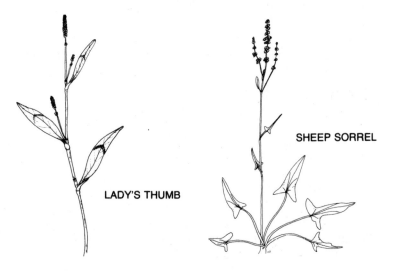

SHEEP SORREL

LADY'S THUMB

Sheep Sorrel, *Rumex acetosella*, is a low-growing, dainty, tiny-flowered plant with two kinds of flower stalks. The yellowish stalks have only stamens, the reddish-flowered stalks produce the pistils. After the pollen is shed, the yellowish stalks shrivel, while the developing wings on the sepals of the reddish flower stalks make them more noticeable. Sorrel is excellent food for grazing animals; the leaves have been used for tanning leather; bits of leaves are useful to flavor fish and rice. Sorrel is found all over the United States, naturalized from Europe.

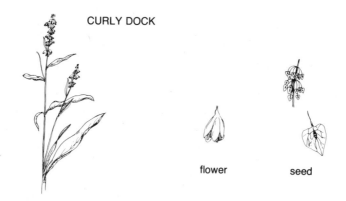

CURLY DOCK

flower   seed

Curly Dock, *Rumex crispus*, is tall-growing (1-2 meters, 3-6 ft), especially noticeable when the red-brown, enlarged sepals have become winged. The fleshy root once was valued as a tonic; young tender leaves can be cooked like spinach and are rich in Vitamin A. A very common weed in valleys and up to 4,500 feet in the mountains all over the United States, naturalized from Europe.

BUTTERCUP or CROWFOOT FAMILY
Ranunculaceae

The members of this family are hard to fit into a pattern. Most have five sepals, but the number of petals varies from zero to sixteen or more. The most dependable characteristic of the family is a cluster of separate pistils on a mound surrounded by many stamens. Various members of the family do not seem to resemble one another until they are examined for this family characteristic. There seem to be exceptions to many of the characteristics: they are herbs, except Clematis is a vine; leaves are palmately divided, alternate, or basal, except Clematis where they are opposite; flowers are complete, parts separate, free and distinct and usually regular (petals all the same shape), except Delphinium; blossoms grow singly, one to a branch, except some are in racemes or panicles; five sepals usually, but always there are more than two, and they may be petal-like as in Clematis and Anemone; the number of stamens varies, even on the same plant; *but* always there are several, separate pistils, the one-celled ovaries superior. The fruit is a pod, an achene, or (rarely) a berry.

All these variations within the same family indicate a very simple, undeveloped kind of plant. Buttercups, well-known wildflowers, are among the earliest flowers in the fossil record—and are also among the earliest flowers found each spring. Other very familiar members are: Anemone, Larkspur, Delphinium, Peony, and Columbine. The flower parts of most are in fives, with separate sepals and petals (though petals are sometimes absent). But remember the best clues: many stamens and many separate pistils on a mound.

Virgin's Bower, *Clematis virginiana,* is a woody vine which grasps fences and trees by its leafstalks. It has opposite, compound leaves, with three oval leaflets. The flowers are white and are borne in clusters. Each flower is about 2.5 cm (1 in) across, and has four spreading petal-like sepals. The many stamens are creamy and give an airiness to the plants. As the flowers fade, each pistil develops into an achene with a long coiling silky plume-like tail. The seed head is even more attractive than the blossoms. This *Clematis* can be found in woods and fence rows from Canada to Georgia and west to Kansas.

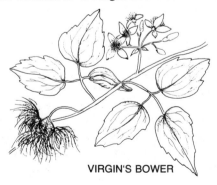

VIRGIN'S BOWER

Bell-rue, Purple Virgin's Bower, *Clematis verticillaris,* is a vine
and has compound leaves. It has large purple or blue flowers
which are very attractive. The four sepals are large and petal-
like, 2.5 cm or longer (1 in). There are many stamens. The
flowers are borne singly, not in clusters as in *C. virginiana.*
Purple Clematis can be found in woods from Canada to Maryland and west to Iowa, blooming in May and June.

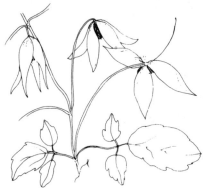

BELL-RUE

LEATHER FLOWER

Leather Flower, Vase-vine, *Clematis viorna,* does not have such
showy flowers as *C. verticillaris.* Its urn-shaped blossoms are
smaller, purplish-brown in color (hence one of its common
names) with only the tips of the four to five sepals turning out.
The vine has opposite leaves with smooth edges. Its fruits produce a great plume of hairy tails which is very attractive. It
grows in woods from Pennsylvania to Georgia and west to
Missouri.

Curl-flower, *Clematis crispa,* is a lovely Clematis having bell-like blue or purple blossoms which are borne singly and are 5 cm long. Like most Clematis, they have four sepals, each with a wavy margin, but no petals. This vine has broad, ovate, heart-shaped leaves, or sometimes leaves may be very narrow on some of these variable plants. Curl-flower grows in swamps from Virginia to Florida to Texas and from Illinois and Missouri south to Arkansas and Tennessee.

Pine-hyacinth, *Clematis baldwinii,* is an erect plant 30-60 cm tall (1-2 ft). There are one to three blue or lavender flowers on each long bare stalk. The basal leaves vary greatly; some are entire, others are divided into very narrow lobes. They can be found in the sandy, pine areas of Florida.

Curly-heads, *Clematis ochroleuca,* is an erect plant 30-60 cm tall (1-2 ft). The single flowers droop on long stalks above the opposite, heart-shaped leaves. There are no petals and the four sepals form a yellowish, urn-shaped blossom. These grow in sandy areas from New York to Georgia.

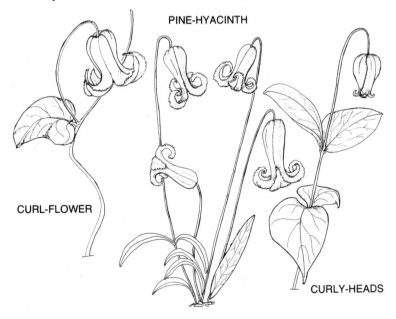

PINE-HYACINTH

CURL-FLOWER

CURLY-HEADS

ANEMONES are one of the loveliest (and often earliest) of spring wildflowers. The sepals are very petal-like; usually there are five, but some have more. A common name for Anemones is Windflower.

Canada Anemone, *Anemone canadensis*, is a showy white flower about 3.5 cm (1.5 in) across, growing on a 30-60 cm tall (1-2 ft) strong plant. It has broad compound leaves, each with three to five toothed leaflets. There are no petals, but the five white sepals are large and petal-like and enclose many yellow stamens and a mound of green pistils. Canada Anemone can be found across Canada and south to Virginia, west to Missouri,

CANADA ANEMONE

and even as far as New Mexico. It blooms from May through July in moist meadows or along streams. It has been cultivated because of its beauty.

Rue Anemone, *Anemonella thalictroides,* is a dainty little flower that is white or pale pink and is borne on the tip of a black stem with an involucre just below the flower. The involucre is really two small leaves, each divided into three parts and each with a long thin stem, so the involucre looks like six small leaves on each flower stalk. There are five to ten sepals, sometimes even more, looking like petals. The many stamens are such a pale yellow they are nearly white. The mound of pistils is a very pale green. The plant is small, only 10-25 cm tall (4-10 in), with black, slender, wiry stems. The lovely leaves are divided into threes with three small leaflets in each division. It blooms in spring all over the east in woodsy places.

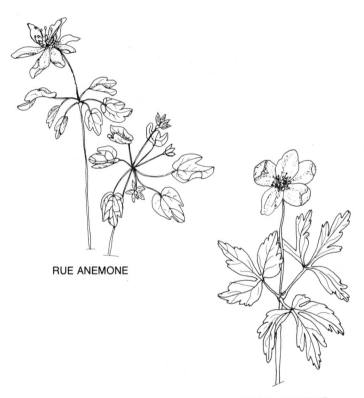

RUE ANEMONE

WOOD ANEMONE

Wood Anemone, *Anemonella quinquefolia,* is the earliest Windflower each spring. It also is the smallest of the wild anemones, being only 10-20 cm tall (4-8 in). The pure white blossoms are seen easily in moist woods and damp meadows from Canada to Georgia and west to Tennessee, from April to June. The five sepals look like satiny petals, with a mass of pale yellow stamens. The leaves are compound, with three sharply toothed leaflets, the side leaflets so deeply cut the leaf seems to have five parts.

Anemone caroliniana is different from most other anemones in that there are many white sepals (instead of just a few), each sepal looking like a petal. There are always at least ten sepals and there may be twice that many. It has a solitary flower on each stem tip. There is an involucre below the middle of the flowering stem and many basal leaves; both are cut into narrow lobes. This little plant grows only about 30 cm tall (12 in) in sandy soil or grassy areas from South Dakota to Florida.

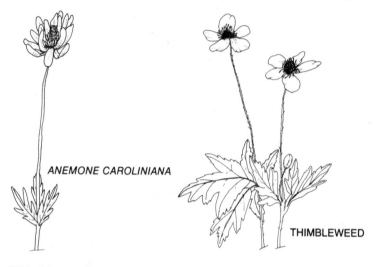

ANEMONE CAROLINIANA

THIMBLEWEED

Thimbleweed, *Anemone virginiana,* grows to be a meter tall (3 ft) on thick, hairy stalks, with a group of large, compound basal leaves. Smaller modified leaves on the flowering stems form involucre-like groups around the stems many centimeters below the blossom. The flower has five petal-like white sepals and many yellow stamens with a tall mound of green pistils. The mound of mature fruits (small achenes) is shaped like a thimble, giving the plant its common name. It grows in open rocky woods from Maine to Georgia, west to Kansas and North Dakota.

Tall Meadow Rue, *Thalictrum polyganum,* grows one to two meters or more (3-7 ft) near ponds or in damp meadows. Many small flowers grow in spreading clusters. There are two kinds of flowers—male (or staminate) flowers with masses of white stamens, and female (or pistillate) flowers which have groups of pistils, sometimes with a few stamens mixed in. The staminate and pistillate flowers are usually on different plants. There are no petals and the greenish sepals fall early. The masses of white stamens in the staminate flowers make an attractive flower. This can be found from Canada to Georgia all summer, and is very common.

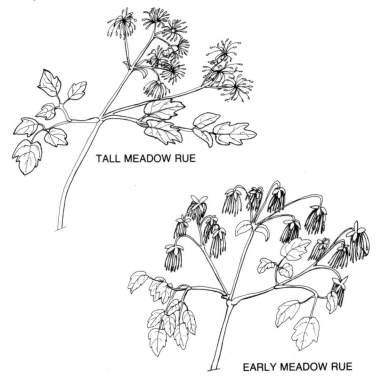

TALL MEADOW RUE

EARLY MEADOW RUE

Early Meadow Rue, *Thalictrum dioicum,* also grows from Canada to Georgia and west to Missouri on streambanks and in the woods. The small, greenish flowers droop in clusters on plants 30-60 cm tall (1-3 ft). There are no petals, but four small purplish sepals. The male and female flowers are on separate plants—the staminate flowers with their many long greenish-yellow stamens are the noticeable plants. The leaves are small and delicate, divided into rounded lobes.

Marsh Marigold or Cowslip, *Caltha palustria,* makes bright spots
of sunny color at edges of swamps, wet meadows, and ponds
from eastern Canada to South Carolina and west to Nebraska
in May and June. There are no petals, but the golden-yellow
sepals make a beautiful flower. The number of sepals varies,
sometimes on the same plant, from three to eight, but most
have five sepals. The flowers are more than 3 cm across (1 in).
There are numerous yellow stamens and several pistils. The
pistils develop into a cluster of pods or-follicles. The hollow
stems are 30-60 cm tall (1-3 ft). They branch, bearing a flower at

MARSH MARIGOLD

the tip of each branch. The leaves are alternate, somewhat
heart-shaped or kidney-shaped with a slightly toothed margin.
Yellow dye can be made from the sepals. The leaves can be
cooked and eaten as greens, but strangely enough are very
poisonous if eaten *raw*. It is a close relative of the common
Cowslip of England.

Round-lobed Liver Leaf, *Hepatica americana,* is a small wood-
land plant found all over the east. The name "round-lobe"
refers to the large, spotted basal leaves that have a three-lobed,
very distinctive shape. The flowers may be white, pink, or
lavender. They have no petals, but the six sepals seem petal-
like. There are many stamens with white or very pale yellow

ROUND-LOBED LIVER LEAF

anthers. Just a short distance down the stem from the flower are three small, unlobed leaves which might be mistaken for sepals; however, they are not attached to the flower, so they aren't sepals, but form an involucre. The stems of both leaves and flowers are noticeably hairy.

Sharp-lobed Hepatica, *Hepatica acutiloba*, has leaf lobes that are pointed (as the scientific name suggests), and larger than those of the Round-lobed Liver Leaf (up to 10 cm across). The leaves of this species are the characteristic, recognizable feature. The hairs on the stem are long and point downwards. Otherwise this Hepatica is much like the Round-lobed Hepatica. It has no petals, but has five to six sepals colored pink, white, or lavender. These, too, grow all over the east.

SHARP-LOBED HEPATICA

ARUM FAMILY
Araceae

This is a family with tiny flowers (which could be mistaken for stamens) packed together around a stalk. Usually a large colored spathe (which could be mistaken for one big petal) envelops the flowers. The most familiar example of this is the Calla Lily of gardens. The little flowers are borne densely on a stalk called a spadix. There are no petals; usually there are four to six sepals but sometimes they, too, are missing. The spathe is wrapped around the base of the spadix. Most members of this family grow on muddy banks or ponds and near streams or in moist woods. This family is mainly tropical, but some are well-known eastern wildflowers. Taro, an important food in the Pacific Islands, belongs to this family.

Skunk-cabbage, *Symplocarpus* (*Spathyema*) *foetidus*, is one of the first plants to bloom in wet woods of the east. The flowers bloom before the leaves are fully opened. As with other members of this family, there are many tiny flowers crowded onto a broad spadix with the large mottled green to purple-brown bulbous spathe around it. The spathe may be quite thick and is often pointed and twisted at the tip. Each tiny flower has four sepals, but no petals. As the flowers fade, the many large cabbage-like leaves with very prominent veins unroll and become the noticeable part of the plant. The fading flowers develop a very objectionable odor, which gives the plant its common name. The leaves may grow to a meter in length. Skunk-cabbage is found from Canada south to Georgia, and west to Iowa. It is edible, but only with many water changes during the boiling process, and by adding baking soda. It must not be confused with the very poisonous Indian Poke (*Veratrum viride*) which it grows with and somewhat resembles. The leaves of Indian Poke are noticeably "pleated," and its greenish flowers are in large branching panicles.

Wild-calla or Water Arum, *Calla palustris*, fills acres of north-eastern swamp land. The blossoms look much like the garden callas, but the spathe is more open. It is white inside but greenish outside. The spadix is shorter than the spathe, and is covered with tiny yellow-green flowers. There are no petals and no sepals, but each flower has six stamens and a pistil. The ovaries ripen into a large head of red berries. The leaves are thick, glossy, and shaped like leaves of garden callas, and are 5-12.5 cm long (2-5 in).

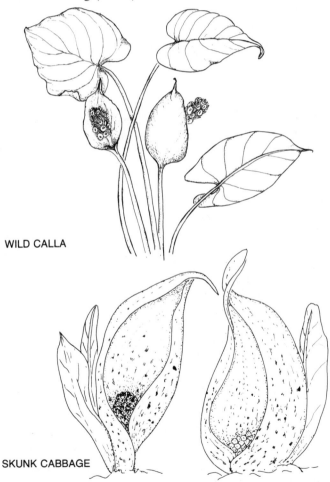

WILD CALLA

SKUNK CABBAGE

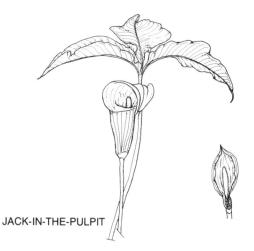

JACK-IN-THE-PULPIT

Jack-in-the-Pulpit, *Arisaema triphyllum*, is a strange little wildflower found in spring in the eastern woods. The plants grow 30-60 cm tall (12-24 in). The tiny flowers are crowded at the base of the green or purple spadix, which is nearly hidden in the spathe. The spathe is striped red-brown and is yellow inside and green with yellow stripes outside. It curves into a broad flap over the spadix, nearly hiding "Jack" as he sits in his "pulpit." There usually are two leaves, each divided into three leaflets, 8-20 cm long (3-8 in). This plant is also called Indian Turnip because the round corms are turnip-like and were eaten by the Indians who boiled them to eat as a vegetable, or dried and ground them into a meal for cakes. All parts of this plant have needle-like crystals of calcium oxalate, so it must be carefully boiled to be edible. This plant has become rather rare in some areas, but is found fairly frequently in the northeast.

SPURGE FAMILY
Euphorbiaceae

This is a family of great variety. Most members grow in the tropics, several are successful desert plants (often resembling cacti), but some are found as common weeds in the east. The blossoms are always small. There are no petals and often no sepals either, and the stamens and pistils are in different flowers. There may be many stamens, but one species has a male flower that consists of just one stamen. There is one pistil with three styles. Usually the flowers are in groups, surrounded by bracts (which may appear petal-like). The flowers are often greenish and most spurges have a milky juice. Well-known members of the family are Tapioca, Castor-oil plants, Rubber trees, and Poinsettias. All have *poisonous* juice, although parts of some plants (like Tapioca and Castor-oil) may be used for food or medicine.

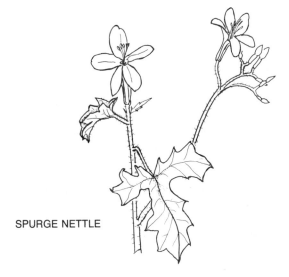

SPURGE NETTLE

Spurge Nettle or Tread Softly, *Cnidoscolus stimulosus,* is an unusually lovely little flower with five waxy white sepals that look like petals. It seems lovely until you touch the stem or leaves. They are covered with long, stiff hairs that sting and can *poison,* causing a painful inflammation. In Mexico it is called "Mala Mujer," meaning "bad woman." It blooms from March through September from Virginia to Texas and into Mexico in swampy areas.

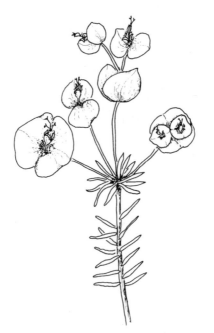

CYPRESS SPURGE

Cypress Spurge, *Euphorbia cyparissias*, is a very common European weed now found in both the northeast and the southeast, growing in dense golden masses. The stiff stems grow to be 60 cm tall (24 in), with the tiny flower clusters grouped in umbels at the ends of the branches, often in pairs. The flowers are noticeable only because of their abundance and the bright greenish-yellow bracts which surround groups of them. These bracts turn reddish as the flower fades. Each tiny flower has four waxy crescent-shaped yellow glands surrounding the stamen or pistil. The three-celled pistil with three branched styles stands on a stalk protruding from the female flower. A hand lens helps show the marvelous intricacy of these minute flowers. The Cypress Spurge blooms from April to August in fields and along roads from Maine to Colorado, and south to North Carolina and Missouri.

Chapter IV

FLOWERS WITH THREE PETALS
(but which may seem to have six)

Most of the flowers that seem to have six sepals really have just three petals in the inside circle and three sepals in the outside circle. The sepals and petals are usually colored alike, thus all masquerading as six petals. It is important to examine the flower to see the *circles*. All flowers that seem to have six petals, but have parallel-veined leaves, really have three petals and three sepals, not six petals.

LILY FAMILY
Liliaceae

In the Lily Family the three petals and three sepals often are not only colored alike but may also be shaped very much alike and all may stand upwards like petals. There are six stamens with the filaments sometimes quite broad or winged. The stigma may have three bumps. The ovary is three-parted and superior. Flowers may be in umbels, racemes, heads, or solitary. All lilies grow from bulbs, corms, or rootstocks. Agricultural plants which are members of this family are asparagus and onions. Garden flowers are the Tiger Lily and Tulip.

Dogtooth Violet or Fawn Lily, *Erythronium americanum,* is one
of the earliest of the lilies too appear in the spring. It is a lily
with all the family characteristics, not at all a Violet. The only
resemblance to a dog's tooth is in the little bulbs which form on
white underground branches. These send up new plants with
only one leaf. For several years single leaves grow with no
flower. When the plants do bloom, they have two broad
parallel-veined leaves which are splotched with brown in most
plants. The flowering stalk is bare, with one lovely little yellow
blossom drooping from its end. The three sepals, which curl
back, are tinged on the outside with brown. The three petals
are narrow and cover the six long brown stamens and the
three-parted style. The stamens are in two circles of three each,
one circle shorter than the other. Dogtooth Violets are very
common from Canada to Florida, where they often make a
mass of growth over large areas. A similiar species called
White Dogtooth Violet, *E. albidum,* has white blooms and
grows from Ontario to Georgia, west to Missouri and Oklahoma.

DOGTOOTH VIOLET   STAR OF BETHLEHEM

Star of Bethlehem, *Ornithogalum umbellatum,* is a plant from
Europe which has escaped into the wild areas from Newfoundland to Mississippi and west to Nebraska. It has three sepals
and three petals, all a beautiful waxy white with a green stripe
up the outside of each. The six stamens form a crown around
the single pistil, each a traingle with the yellow anthers making
the "jewels." All parts of this plant are said to be *poisonous.*

Dogberry or Corn-Lily, *Clintonnia borealis*, is a yellow wood lily, with three to eight flowers in an umbel on a 15-23 cm (6-15 in) plant. Each flower has three greeni sh-yellow sepals, three greenish-yellow petals, and six stamens. The flower is about two and a half centimeters long. The fruits are shiny, dark blue berries, which give the plant its common name. The two or three large basal leaves are glossy green, and are oval or oblong. These grow from Newfoundland to North Carolina and to Wisconsin. They carpet woodlands in northern New York. White Clintonia, *Clintonia umbellulata*, is very similar, except that it has small, speckled white flowers. It grows in woods from New York to Georgia.

FALSE SOLOMON'S SEAL

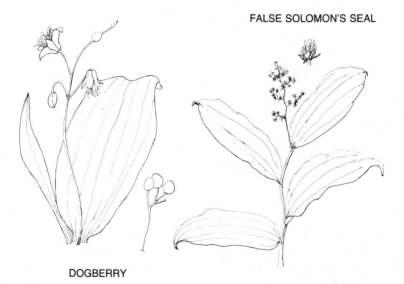

DOGBERRY

False Solomon's Seal, *Smilacina racemosa*, has leaves that are very noticeable. They are 7.5-15 cm long (3-6 ine) and 2.5-7.5 cm (1-3 in) wide—wider than most lilies—with wavy margins and a fresh green color. They are conspicuously parallel veined and sessile on the zigzag stalk. The flowers are tiny—1 cm (.5 in) wide or less. Both petals and sepals are white. The flowers grow in a dense terminal raceme about 5 cm long. The fruit is a red berry. This plant is found in moist woods all over America.

Hairy Solomon's Seal, *Polygonatum biflorum*, the beautifully veined, wavy-margined, somewhat oval leaves grow alternately along the somewhat zigzag stem. The greenish-white flowers usually are in pairs nodding from the leaf axils. They are shaped like a long tube ending in six lobes, giving a bell-like appearance. A larger species, *Polygonatum canaliculatum*, has two to ten flowers 1-2.5 cm long (.5-1 in) on curved, rather than bent, stalks. These grow from Canada to Florida and Texas.

HAIRY SOLOMON'S SEAL

TWISTED STALK

Twisted Stalk or White Mandarin, *Streptopus amplexifolius*, not only has a twisted or zigzag stem which is more exaggerated than most Solomon's Seals, but it has one unique characteristic which gives it the name of Twisted Stalk—the flower's stem is twisted! Instead of growing from the axil of the leaf, as in many flowers, it grows from the side of the stem away from the leaf, then twists back under the leaf. Then a single flower, 1 cm (.5 in) long, hangs from that twisted stem at a right angle. The base of the leaf is also different in this species—it extends around the stem to the opposite side from where it is attached. The plants may be 90 cm tall (3 ft). They grow from Greenland and Labrador to Alaska, then south, especially in New York and the mountains further south.

Wild Onion, *Allium cernuum*, grows on roadsides and in fields from New York to the Carolinas and westward to Oregon. The bulbs and leaves have a very strong onion odor and were used by Indians and pioneers for flavoring food. The many pinkish-purple or white flowers grow in an umbel on top of a slender stem, making a very beautiful blossom. The flower cluster is enclosed by two bracts; these may drop off early. Each small flower has the usual lily pattern—three sepals and three petals colored alike, either pink or pinkish-lavender. The six anthers are yellow, and grow on long slender filaments, giving the whole flower an airy grace. The leaves are very narrow.

Wild Chives, *Allium sibiricum*, is another very similar flower, but this one has hollow leaves, shorter than the flower stem, like the garden onion. It grows to 60 cm (24 in) tall, with the flowers clustered at the top of the slender stem in a head and is at first enclosed by two pinkish bracts. It is found in New England and all across the northern part of America to the Pacific coast. It, too, can be used for flavoring food.

Wild Garlic, *Allium canadense*, also has edible bulbs. It grows so thickly in some areas its leaves look like a field of grass. This is especially true in Arkansas, but they grow abundantly from Maine to Florida, to South Dakota, and to Texas in open fields, woods, meadows, and prairies. The leaves are narrow and grasslike, the flowers are small, growing in a head on a slender stalk. The flower heads are enclosed by two to three broad bracts. The flowers have three sepals and three petals, all pink, and six stamens. It is a beautiful flower.

WILD ONION

WILD CHIVES

WILD GARLIC

Wild Hyacinth, *Camassia scilloides*, is an especially lovely flower, growing in loose clusters on a 30-60 cm (12-24 in) long stalk. The pale lavender-blue flowers have the sepals and petals colored alike; the pistil and stamens are yellow. Long, very slender leaves grow about half as tall as the flower stalk. Wild Hyacinths can be found in the spring from Pennsylvania to Alabama and westward. It is a close relative of the lovely Blue Camass of the west.

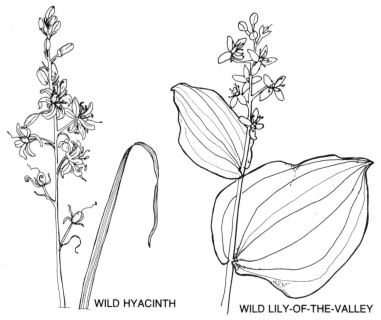

WILD HYACINTH   WILD LILY-OF-THE-VALLEY

Wild Lily-of-the-Valley or Canada Mayflower, *Maianthemum (Unifolium) canadense*, grows in great masses in the woods of Canada and Maine, and south to Georgia, west to Iowa. The blossoms are small but the many clusters of tiny flowers and the glossy, beautiful leaves make a mass of beauty. They are not typical lilies, for they only have two sepals, two petals, four stamens, and a two-parted ovary. They are low-growing plants with the flowering stalks growing from slender underground stems. The flowering stalk has two heart-shaped clasping leaves. They flower from May through June. The fruit is a speckled berry, greenish or brown, which slowly turns red.

Wood Lily, *Lilium philadelphicum*, is a bright, always noticed lily. The plant grows 40-90 cm tall (24-36 in). Usually there is a single bright orange-red blossom borne erect, but occasionally there may be several. Each flower is 7.5-10 cm (3-4 in) across, and has the typical lily arrangement of three sepals, three petals, six stamens and one pistil. The petals and sepals are orange or red, yellowish at the base and splotched with dark brown. They are very narrow at the base, not overlapping as many lilies. The stamens and pistil are also colorful. Slender, pointed, parallel-veined leaves are in whorls up the stem. Wood Lilies grow from Canada to North Carolina and west as far as Kentucky.

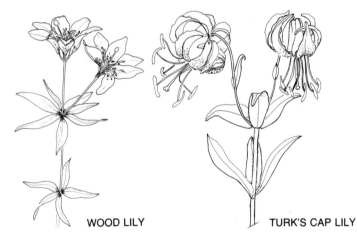

WOOD LILY   TURK'S CAP LILY

Turk's Cap Lily, *Lilium superbum*, is a spectacular sight. Sometimes as many as fifty large bright blossoms nod on a 1.5-2.5 meter (5-7 ft) tall plant. The three sepals and three petals are brilliant orange-red and spotted with darker red. They curl backwards over the stem exposing the six long stamens with red anthers and yellow filaments, and the one long pistil with its red stigma and yellow style, all of which hang below the nodding flowers. The lower leaves are in whorls around the stout stem, the upper leaves growing in pairs or scattered. This lily grows from Canada to Florida and westward to Missouri. Carolina Lily, *Lilium michauxii*, is a very similar species found from the Carolinas to Louisiana.

Daylily, *Hemerocallis fulva*, actually is a garden flower which has escaped to the wild, but is so abundant along roads and in woods over much of the east that it is now one of the most common wildflowers. The typical lily blossoms are 10-12 cm (4-5 in) across, funnel-shaped, and colored red-orange. The leaves are basal, quite long and narrow. The naked flower stalks may be .75-1.5 meters (24-48 in) tall. They branch several times near the top, each branch bearing several flowers, each opening only for a few hours or a day. Buds keep opening on successive days, so during the season there are always some flowers, some buds, some withered flowers. A yellow species, *Hemerocallis flava*, also can be found; it does not grow as tall.

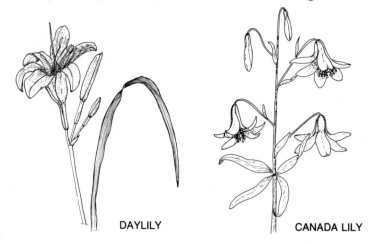

DAYLILY

CANADA LILY

Canada Lily or Wild Yellow Lily, *Lilium canadense*, is a spectacular flower with several large nodding blossoms growing at the end of a 60-150 cm (2-5 ft) stem. There sometimes are as many as twenty blossoms on one stem. The petals and sepals all are colored alike; usually they are yellow, but they may be orange or red, always with dark spots. Each flower hangs from its stem and is somewhat bell-shaped, the petal and sepal tips curving away from the six dark red or brown stamens. The lower leaves on the stalk are in whorls. This lovely lily is found in moist meadows and open woods from Canada to Alabama, to Minnesota, blooming all summer. In the south they usually are found in mountainous or hilly areas.

Bellwort, *Uvularia perfoliata*, is a small yellow lily with the base of the leaf growing around the stem so the stem seems to pierce the long, pointed leaves. They are smooth and parallel-veined with a whitish bloom. The bright yellow little flowers are drooping; the petals seem to twist curiously, their three sepals and three petals shaped much alike. They may be 15-25 cm (6-10 in) tall. They bloom from April to June in woods from Canada to the Gulf of Mexico, and are especially abundant in the Maine woods.

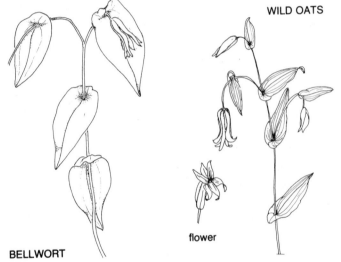

WILD OATS

flower

BELLWORT

Large-flowered Bellwort, *Uvularia grandiflora*, has bright yellow flowers, somewhat larger than those of *U. perfoliata*—both the petals and leaves tend to twist in this species—more so than in *U. perfoliata*. Otherwise, they look much alike. These, too, are flowers of the woods all over the east.

Wild Oats or Merry Bells, *Uvularia sessilifolia*, has sessile leaves, as the name indicates. They are alternate along the slender stem, which grows 25-35 cm tall (10-14 in). There are dainty little pale yellow flowers, long and narrow, drooping downwards. They bloom April to June in woods from Canada into New England, and in mountains all over the east, and as far west as Oklahoma.

TRILLIUMS are different from other lilies in that they have netted-veined leaves. Three large green leaves grow in a whorl around the stout unbranched stem just below the solitary three-petal flower. Trilliums are among the first spring flowers all over America and in many places are protected by law because if the flower is picked the perennial rootstalk will die. The only leaves are those three located just under the flower, so no food can be made or stored if the leaves are gone. The sepals are three in number, and usually are greenish, though they may be somewhat colored.

Stinking Benjamin, or Red Trillium, *Trillium erectum*, is the most common eastern trillium. It is a dark, purplish-red flower with three petals about 3 cm (1.5 in), three greenish sepals, and long purplish stamens. Sometimes the flower is greenish or whitish also. It stands on a 10 cm stalk above the leaves. The purple ovary has three curved spreading styles. It develops into a six-lobed reddish berry about 2 cm thick. This trillium can be found from Canada to North Carolina and Tennessee from April to May. The common name comes from its unpleasant odor.

STINKING BENJAMIN

LARGE-FLOWERED WHITE TRILLIUM

Large-flowered White Trillium, *Trillium grandiflorum*, is a fabulous flower which grows 20-45 cm tall (8-18 in) in moist woods from Canada to North Carolina and Missouri. The pure white flower is 5-7.5 cm across (2-3 in). Its three petals spread upwards. They are strongly veined and are much longer than the three green sepals. The flower stands above the leaves on a long stalk. The six stamens have yellow anthers about one cm long, making it an outstandingly beautiful trillium.

Dwarf White Trillium, or Snow Trillium, *Trillium nivale*, is a tiny trillium only 10-12.5 cm (4-5 in) tall. The leaves are narrow and oval, about 2 cm long. They bloom in March and April from Pennsylvania to Kentucky and into the Midwest.

DWARF WHITE TRILLIUM

Yellow Trillium, *Trillium luteum*, grows 20-30 cm (8-12 in) tall
with three large, spotted leaves. The slender, yellow-petalled
flower sits right above the big leaves, the petals standing erect;
they are lemon-scented. These are found in the southern Appalachian Mountains in April and May.

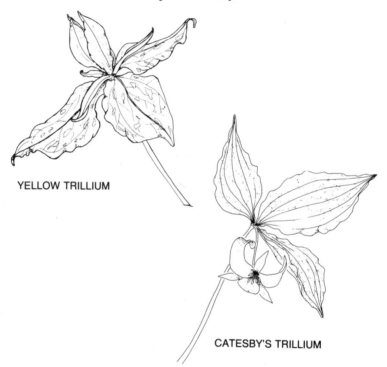

YELLOW TRILLIUM

CATESBY'S TRILLIUM

Catesby's Trillium, *Trillium catesbaei*, has light pinkish blossoms which frequently are pink-lavender when they age. The
plants are 25-30 cm (10-12 in) tall, with the three sessile leaves
at the top of the stem quite wavy-edged and their five main
veins very prominent. The three sepals are green and much
narrower and somewhat shorter than the three petals. The
flowers are on bent stems so they hang sideways or even below
the leaves. The stamens are bright yellow. Acres of these grow
in the northern woods, but are rather rare in the southern Ap-
palachians, blooming in May.

Painted Trillium, *Trillium undulatum*, has three white (or pink-ish) petals with a V-shaped spot of crimson or magenta veins near the base. They are somewhat slender and longer than the three green sepals, and have wavy margins. The six stamens are long and yellow with pink tips, the three slender styles spreading. The ovary ripens into a three-angled bright red shiny berry. It is a very striking trillium, common in moist woods from Canada to Georgia in May.

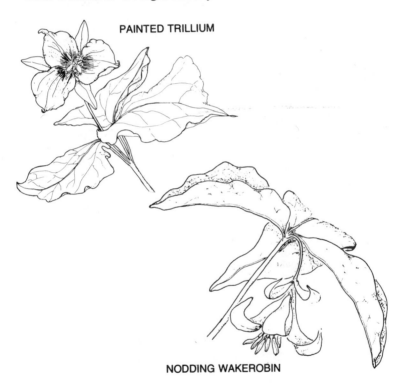

PAINTED TRILLIUM

NODDING WAKEROBIN

Nodding Wakerobin, *Trillium cernuum*, grows 20-50 cm tall (8-20 in). The white or very pale pink flower is about 2.5 cm across (1 in), and droops below the three large leaves (up to 15 cm long). The petals are very waxy and curve back, exposing the six pink stamens and the whitish or pink stigma. The ovary ripens into a red-purple berry. This trillium is found throughout the east, flowering in May and June.

AMARYLLIS FAMILY
Amaryllidaceae

Members of this family are much like lilies except they have inferior ovaries, and the lower part of the sepals and petals may be joined to form a tube. The flowers may be arranged along the stem or may be in umbels. The six stamens are attached to the inside of the corolla tube. These are perennial plants growing from bulbs, corms, or rootstocks. The leaves are narrow, often grass-like, with parallel veins. The flowers have three colored sepals and three colored petals, all looking very much alike, but in two "circles." Narcissus and daffodils are members of this family.

Florida Swamp-Lily, *Crinum americanum*, is a lovely white amaryllis with long, narrow spreading sepals and petals, joined about halfway down into a long tube. Several flowers bloom on a single stem. They grow in wet areas along the coast from Florida to Texas.

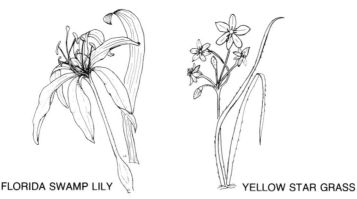

FLORIDA SWAMP LILY   YELLOW STAR GRASS

Yellow Star Grass, *Hypoxis hirsuta*, blooms from early spring all through the summer, and its lily-like little yellow flowers shine out of meadows like golden stars among the grass. Their leaves are long, narrow, and hairy, and nearly hide the cluster of blossoms which may be only 10-12.5 cm (4-5 in) tall. They grow all over the east.

Atamasco Lily, Zephyr Lily, *Zephyranthes atamasco*, is a beautiful white or pinkish flower about 6 cm (2.5 in) across, much like an Easter Lily in general appearance. The sepals and petals are quite broad, not tapered. The long yellow anthers of the six stamens contrast beautifully with the white petals and sepals. The leaves are long, sharp-edged, and narrow. This flower can be found from Florida to Mississippi and north to Virginia. Atamasco is an Indian word—supposedly they used it for toothaches.

ATAMASCO LILY

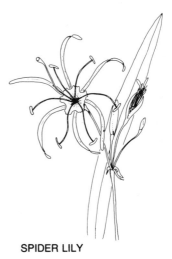

SPIDER LILY

Spider Lily, *Hymenocallis occidentalis*, grows along the coast of South Carolina to southern Florida and Louisiana and in bogs and meadows north to Georgia, Kentucky, and Missouri. This fragrant flower is most unusual in appearance, having three very long, slender sepals and three identical-appearing petals. The six stamens and one pistil also are extremely long. All together they give the flower its common name. There is also an unusual thin, notched tissue or "crown" which connects the base of the stamens, forming a cup somewhat like that of narcissus, a relative of this plant. The flowers grow in umbels of three to six blossoms on a leafless stalk. The numerous leaves are basal, quite thick, and up to 60 cm long (2 ft). They are whitish, with a "bloom."

IRIS FAMILY
Iridaceae

Iris flower parts are in threes, as are lilies and amaryllis. One important difference is that a lily has a superior ovary; iris and amaryllis have inferior ovaries. But both those other families have six stamens; iris has only three, often hiding under the expanded, 3-parted petal-like stigma. Iris usually grow from thick creeping rootstocks. They have stout stems and grass- or sword-like leaves that straddle the stem or seem to fold around it. Most of the wild iris have a shape similar to that of the garden iris, with the three sepals standing outwards or hanging down (often called "falls") and usually larger or marked differently from the three petals which stand up (and are called the "standards.") Wild iris grow all over America; one species is the state flower of Tennessee; garden Crocus, Gladiolus, and Freesia all belong to this family.

NARROW BLUE FLAG

Narrow Blue Flag, *Iris prismatica*, is a very slender, graceful flower. The blue flowers are veined with yellow, the petals and sepals spreading rather far apart. The leaves are very narrow, almost grass-like. It is common along the coast from Maine to Delaware, growing in wet meadows or swamps of brackish water.

Crested Dwarf Iris, *Iris cristata*, is an especially lovely little iris, recognizable because of the yellow crest, which is a "pleated" projection standing up on each of the falls. The flower is a rich blue, light purple, or white. The flowering stem is only 10-15 cm (4-6 in) tall, with thick, sheathing leaves. When in bloom, the Crested Iris produces a mass of blue on open banks and roadsides. The leaves are stout and may grow to 30 cm (1 ft) in length after the blooming period. Grows in woods from Maryland to Georgia, and westward to Missouri.

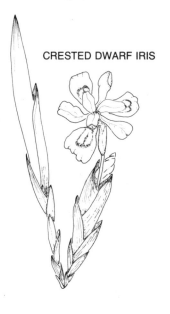

CRESTED DWARF IRIS

COMMON BLUE FLAG

Common Blue Flag or Poison Flag, *Iris versicolor*, grows abundantly along ponds and streams and in wet meadows from Canada and New England to Virginia and west to Minnesota and Ohio. The beautiful blue-purple flower is about 7.5 cm across (3 in). The long falls are generally heavily veined with dark blue lines, quite pale at the base. The flower stalks may be 60-90 cm (24-36 in) tall. The slender, fairly short leaves form a dense mass along stream borders. The rootstock is extremely *poisonous*.

Red Iris, *Iris fulva*, is a southern iris growing in marshes and wet fields of Alabama and Georgia. It is a brownish-red or various shades of orange or pinkish. The flowers grow in a 1-1.5 meter (3-5 ft) stalk, with a cluster of flowers to each stalk. Each flower is wide open, with three broad sepals, three smaller petals and the peculiar petal-like stigmas more or less all colored alike and distinctly veined. All these are united into a long tube above the inferior ovary. It is a fabulous sight to see a mass of these lovely flowers growing in a dark swamp.

RED IRIS

BLUE-EYED GRASS

Blue-eyed Grass, *Sisyrinchium*. There are many species of Blue-eyed Grass growing in masses or sparingly along road-sides and in fields of the east. It is a grass-like plant with the characteristic overlapping, narrow, flat, iris leaves. The dainty star-like flowers are about one cm broad (.5 in), and are a deep blue-purple. They open widely with the petals alternately over-lapping the broader sepals. The three stamens stand erect in the center surrounding the pistil. Several flowers and buds can be found at the top of the slender grass-like flat stems.

ORCHID FAMILY
Orchidaceae

The Orchids are considered exotic flowers, and they are strangely beautiful and delicate. There are three colored sepals all alike, or nearly alike (sometimes the lower two are fused together), and three petals not alike. Usually the lower petal, called the lip, is different from the other two in size, or shape, or color; sometimes it is different in all three ways. Most orchids have only one stamen, but the Lady's Slippers have two. The stamen is united with the style and stigma, forming a column in the center of the flower. This column is often colored. The pollen is in two to eight pear-shaped masses united by elastic threads. The ovary is inferior, three-angled, and usually long. The leaves are parallel veined and sheathing.

Orchids may grow on trees with no roots in the ground. They are not parasites, but use the trees for support, and receive their nourishment from the moist air. Such orchids are called epiphytes; most of them grow in the tropics, but we have some of them in the semi-tropical areas of Florida and around the Gulf of Mexico. Other orchids grow with roots in the ground, usually in swamps or very moist areas. There are several species of the terrestrial orchids all over the east, especially the strange Lady's Slipper in which the lower petal is greatly enlarged and is pouch or slipper-shaped. In these there are two stamens—one on each side of the column, with a sterile, shield-shaped one at the tip of the column. The lower two sepals of most Lady's Slippers are at least partly joined.

Yellow Lady's Slipper, Downy Lady's Slipper, *Cypripedium calceolus*, grows widely in the northeastern states, west to British Columbia and Washington. It is a terrestrial orchid growing about 60 cm (2 ft) tall in bogs, swamps and damp woody areas. The large, sessile, downy leaves are 7-15 cm long (3-6 in), and up to 7 cm wide (3 in). There are usually one to two flowers on a plant with two to five leaves. The lip may be cream colored to yellow, sometimes with purple lines; inside are white jointed hairs. The long narrow side petals and wider sepals twist, and are greenish-yellow to brownish-purple. This is a variable species and *C. pubescens* (large flowers) and *C. parviflorum* (small flowers) are now just considered varieties.

YELLOW LADY'S SLIPPER

SHOWY LADY'S SLIPPER

Showy Lady's Slipper, *Cypripedium reginae,* is an unusually lovely large wild orchid. The plants may be 30-90 cm tall (1-3 ft), and produce one to three flowers. The lip is pinkish-white with purple streaks and is more than 3 cm (1 in) long. The side petals and the broad sepals are white. The upper sepal arches over the column and the "slipper"; the lower two sepals are fused into one broad one. The leaves are quite large (10-20 cm, 4-8 in), and conspicuously ribbed or pleated. The whole plant is hairy. It grows in cool swamps from Newfoundland to North Carolina, west in the Mountains of Georgia, Tennessee, and Missouri.

Moccasin Flower, Pink Lady's Slipper, *Cypripedium acaule,* has a long, drooping, inflated, cleft lip with the edges rolled inward until they touch (so it's shaped more like a "moccasin" than a "slipper"). It is pink with heavy, deep pink veins; rarely the lip is white. The two sepals (the lower ones are fused) and the two lateral petals are greenish-brown or greenish-purple, and are about 5-8 cm long (2-3 in). The flower is fragrant. The two oval basal leaves, 20 cm long (8 in) are glossy and with very distinctive longitudinal parallel veins. This orchid grows in sandy woods, but also in bogs, from Newfoundland to Alberta and south to Minnesota, Georgia, and Alabama.

MOCCASIN FLOWER

HABENARIA are truly O.   hey are so tiny you must really look at them clos y. The small greenish, yellowish, or whitish flo rs, eac vith a slender spur, are in a long, small-leafed s e. The ower or basal leaves are larger. Many of the Habenarias are delicately fragrant. They are also commonly called Rein Orchids.

Tall Leafy Green Orchid, *Habenaria* (*Limnorchis*) *hyperborea*, has small, fragrant greenish-white flowers in a spike on a stout stem with many narrow leaves. The sepals and petals spread. The smooth-edged lip tapers to a point and is only about 1.5 cm (½ in) long. The spur is about the same size. This orchid grows in swamps, wet cool woods, and along damp roadsides and meadows throughout Canada, southward in the mountains in the east and west, and often very abundantly in the northeast, flowering from May to July.

YELLOW FRINGED
ORCHID

TALL LEAFY GREEN ORCHID

Yellow Fringed Orchid, Orange-Plume, *Habenaria ciliaris*, is a showy orchid because of the mass of small yellowish or orangish blossoms, each on a long stalk, growing in a spike at the top of a slender, 30-80 cm (24-30 in) tall plant. Each bud looks like a little ball on the end of its long stalk. There will be open flowers and buds crowded together in the spike. The three sepals curve back, the two lateral petals are smaller and toothed, the lip very fringed and delicate-appearing. The 2.5-3 cm (1+ in) long slender spur is behind this unique, beautiful lip. The pointed lower leaves are quite large (10-20 cm, 4-8 in), the upper ones along the stalk quite small. Fringed Orchid grows in meadows and open woods, bogs, and in sandy soil from Vermont to Florida to Texas.

Green Fringed Orchid, Ragged Fringed Orchid, *Habernaria lacera*, is a common, small, yellow-green fringed orchid all over the east and as far west as Minnesota, growing in swamps, wet meadows, and woods, flowering in June and July. It may grow 30-100 cm (12-36 in) tall, the stem varying in stoutness. The flowers are in a loose spike with small interspersed leaves. The grooved green inferior ovary is very noticeable in this species and is longer than the spur. The side petals are slender—about the same size as the sepals. The lip is divided into three parts, each deeply fringed. The curved spur is about 2 cm long (.75 in), and is thicker at the end. The lower leaves are fairly slender, from 7.5-20 cm (3-8 in) long. White Fringed Orchid (*H. blephariglottis*) and Purple Fringed Orchid (*H. psycodes*) are similar enough so they are recognizable as orchids in the *Habenaria* genus—all small but lovely.

GREEN FRINGED
ORCHID

ROSE POGONIA

Rose Pogonia, Snake-Mouth, *Pogonia ophioglossoides*, is a common slender orchid up to 36 cm (15 in) tall, usually with only one blossom, and often with only one smallish leaf about halfway up the stem. There may be one or two slender bracts just below the fragrant rose-pink flower. The two side petals and the three sepals are quite narrow and very similar—about 2 cm long, and open widely. The lip is flat, fringed, and has three rows of colored (yellow, white, or brown) hairs. The whole flower is from 2.5-5 cm wide (1-2 in). Rose Pogonia is found frequently all over the east, from southern Canada south from Minnesota to Florida, and west along the coast to Texas.

Ladies'-tresses, *Spiranthes* (*Ibidium*) *cernua*, are orchids with the closely packed flowers growing in a tight spike, often spiralling around the stem or lined up on one side. The flowers have no spurs. There are many species of these little orchids growing all over America, and can also be found on all continents except Africa. The flowers are small and most of them are white, or white with pale yellow lips, often crinkled at the tip. Many of the species have grass-like, basal leaves, which often wither early. The different species are similiar enough to be recognized as Ladies'-tresses, differing slightly with leaf shape, and flower spike arrangement. Some species have very minute flowers, many have flowers in which the petals and sepals are more or less joined or stuck together to form a "hood" over the central column. They may bloom very early in low altitudes in the south, late in the summer in the north.

Butterfly Orchid, *Epidendrum tampense*, is one of the few orchids in our country which grow on trees with its roots in the air. It grows only in Florida in the subtropical forests. The fragrant flowers are greenish-yellow, tinged with purple. The slender sepals and side petals are colored alike. The whitish lip is three-lobed, with two narrow side lobes and a rounded middle lobe that is striped with pink. It is the most common of the *Epidendrum* orchids in our country.

Rattlesnake Plantain, *Goodyera tesselata*, is one of several orchids called Rattlesnake Plantain because the white geometric markings on the basal leaves are somewhat like the markings on a rattlesnake's skin; it is not a plantain, but apparently the flower spike reminded someone of the plantains. A few small leaves grow alternately up the flowering stalk which is topped by a loose spike of small greenish-white flowers. The upper sepal is joined by its edges to the two lateral petals, forming a tiny "hood," the tip of it just turned up. The small, sac-like lip has a tiny "spout" at the end. The flowers tend to spiral up the spike, somewhat like the Ladies'-tresses. It grows from Canada to New York and west to Wisconsin, often in mossy coniferous woods.

LADIES'-TRESSES

BUTTERFLY ORCHID

RATTLESNAKE PLANTAIN

71

SPIDERWORT FAMILY
Commelinaceae

Spiderworts or Dayflowers may be confused with Lilies because their flower parts are in threes and their leaves are parallel-veined. However, Spiderwort leaves are generally folded lengthwise or channeled. The upper ones form a type of spathe below the flower cluster. The stems have definite nodes (they will usually root at those spots), with green-veined membranous sheaths below each leaf. The three sepals are green (not colored similar to the petals as in most Lilies). The fragile petals are primarily blue or purplish (some may be white or pinkish). The six stamens (three of them may be sterile) have very hairy filaments, and the sepals themselves often have glandular hairs. The flowers are usually in clusters at the ends of the branches, often with only one or two flowers open at a time, wither soon, and are replaced by opening buds. In some of the species, the lower petal is smaller and lighter colored. Wandering-Jew, a common house plant, is a member of this family.

Spiderwort or Spider Lily, *Tradescantia virginiana*, is not a Lily, in spite of a common name. It is a beautiful flower but fades soon after blooming—it is open only for a morning. Several unusually lovely blue flowers grow at the top of a 30-90 cm (1-3 ft) stem. Each flower has three separate petals all alike, each about 2.5 cm (1 in) wide, and three tiny, green, hairy sepals. There are six stamens with hairy, deep blue filaments and large yellow anthers. The very tiny, single pistil is green. below the flower cluster is a pair of leaf-like bracts or spathes. The parallel-veined leaves are about 30 cm (12 in) long, about 2 cm (.75 in) wide, and the 2 sides fold upwards. Spiderwort grows in woods from New England to Minnesota, south to Missouri, Tennessee, and Georgia, flowering from April to August, depending on the location.

Dayflower, *Commelina communis*, is so named because its blossoms last just a short time. They are a lovely blue color, but
their three petals are not all alike; two petals stand erect, the
lower one is smaller and usually whitish. The flowers are about
2.5 cm across (1 in). There are three fertile stamens (with pollen), one of which curves inward and has a larger anther than
the other two. The three shorter stamens are sterile but have
tips that are cross-shaped. The three sepals are green. Below
the flower is a lengthwise folded bract or spathe. The many
leaves are about 12.5 cm (5 in) long, about 2 cm wide, and
somewhat fuzzy. This plant is from Asia and has become a
weed. The stem lies on the ground, rooting at each leaf node.
Cut pieces will do the same. It is found commonly in vacant
lots and abandoned areas from Massachusetts to Wisconsin to
Nebraska south to North Carolina, Alabama, Arkansas and
Kansas.

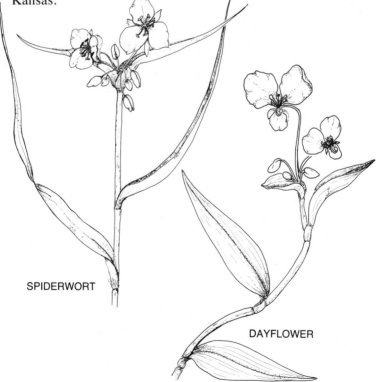

SPIDERWORT

DAYFLOWER

BALSAM FAMILY
Balsaminaceae

This family is most abundant in tropical Africa and Asia but there are some delightful species in the east. The common name, Touch-me-not, comes from the fact that there is a triggering mechanism which snaps the slender ripe capsule open when it is touched, shooting the seeds out; the capsule segments twist in coils as it "shoots." The flowers are irregular. There are three sepals, the two lateral ones are small and green, the lower one petal-like in color and prolonged into a sac-like or bell-like shape with a curly-que end or spur. The slender stalk thus attaches about midway on the flower, so it seems to sort of float in space. From the mouth of this spur come the "five" petals, but really there are only three, for the two lower ones are two-cleft into unequal lobes. The five stamens are short, their filaments more or less united. The simple, alternate leaves are coarsely toothed, the stem juicy and appearing translucent. These plants are abundant in moist spots.

Spotted or Orange Touch-me-not, Impatience, Jewelweed, Snapweed, *Impatiens capensis (biflora)*, is a tall-growing, succulent plant to two and a half meters (5 ft) tall, the foliage more or less purplish. The orange, spotted flowers are about 2.5 cm (1 in) long, and seem to hang horizontally from their midriff on slender stalks. The large saccate sepal is colored and spotted reddish-brown like the petals, the narrow spur long and curving. The three petals (appearing somewhat like five lobes until you look carefully) have the two side petals deeply divided into unlike lobes. The large sepal seems to hold the petals. The toothed leaves are thin, 2.5-7.5 cm long (1-3 in), arranged alternately on the juicy stems. The oblong capsule explodes violently when touched (when ripe), the segments coiling. Found in roadside ditches, moist spots and along creeks from Newfoundland to Alaska, southeast to Florida and Nebraska.

Pale Touch-me-not, *Impatiens pallida,* is similar to *I. capensis,* but the leaves are lighter green, the flowers are pale yellow and larger (to 1.5 cm), and generally only spotted in the throat. The saccate sepal abruptly narrows to a short, curling spur. Will be found from southern Canada to Georgia, west to Kansas, in damp, moist areas.

SPOTTED TOUCH-ME-NOT

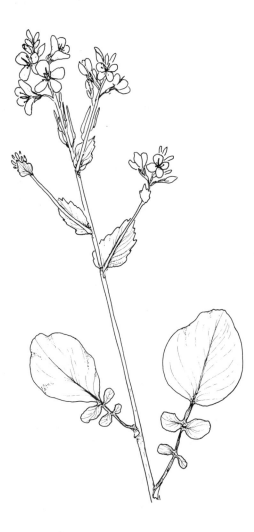

Chapter V

FLOWERS WITH FOUR
SEPARATE PETALS

There are many eastern wildflowers with four petals. Some of them have four separate petals, some have four petals which are at least partly fused or united. We have included the families that are most common in the east, plus Lark-spurs in the Buttercup Family, for they have four petals while most of the members of that family have five petals (or no petals).

MUSTARD FAMILY
Cruciferae

The Mustard Family gets its Latin name from the shape of its small flowers. There are four petals arranged in the shape of a cross, with the base of the petal (claw) quite narrow, the upper part (blade) wider and spreading out to make the four arms of the cross. The four sepals are green or yellow-green, in some species swollen or sac-like, look-ing like a vase holding the four petals. There are six sta-mens, usually with two shorter than the other four. The ovary is superior, with one style, and a one- or two-lobed stigma. The fruit is a two-celled capsule which is usually long and narrow, but may be short and rounded. The seeds are tiny and numerous. Different members of the family have very different types of leaves, and the flowers may be different colors. It is a very widespread family of small plants, typically somewhat pungent.

Bulbous Cress, Bitter Cress, Spring Cress, *Cardamine bulbosa,* has small white flowers about 2 cm (.75 in) across, growing in a loose terminal cluster. The plant grows about 30 cm (1 ft) tall with a slender, rarely branched stem. The leaves are of two kinds: those on the stalk are oblong and sessile and have a few teeth or the margin may be entire, while the basal leaves are round or oval and have long blades, or may even be heart-shaped at the base. Basal leaves are 5 cm across (2 in). There is a cluster of small round corms at the base of the stem. The plant grows from Canada to Florida and west to Minnesota and Texas in wet meadows and other damp spots.

BULBOUS CRESS

Cut-leafed Toothwort or Pepperroot, *Dentaria laciniata* is a dainty little flower growing in woodsy places all over the east. There is a broad raceme of pink or white flowers, each about 2 cm (.75 in) across. The leaves are very characteristic, for they are arranged in whorls of three, with each leaf itself being deeply 3-parted and toothed. They are 5-12 cm (2-5 in) long. The Two-leaved Toothwort, (*D. diphylla*) has very similar flowers but the deeply divided 3-parted toothed leaves are *opposite* each other (instead of 3-whorled). The lobes are also wider. The Large Toothwort (*D. maxima*) has flowers and leaves similar to *D. diphylla* but the leaves are *alternately* arranged and are still wider-lobed. These Toothworts are fairly common from Canada to Kentucky, west to Minnesota, and are found growing in rich woods.

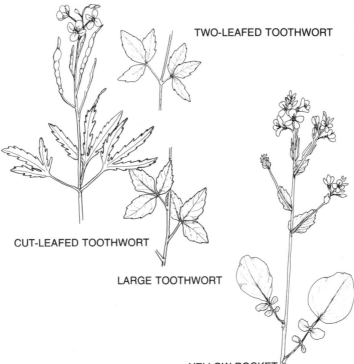

TWO-LEAFED TOOTHWORT

CUT-LEAFED TOOTHWORT

LARGE TOOTHWORT

YELLOW ROCKET

Yellow Rocket or Winter Cress, *Barbarea vulgaris,* is a common field plant especially in damp meadows all over the east, often making many acres yellow with its blossoms. The small flowers are very similar to the true mustards (*Brassica*). The leaves are the distinguishing feature of this cress. The upper leaves are broad, glossy, deeply cut, somewhat fan-shaped, and clasp the stem. The lower leaves have a large end lobe and two to four rounded side lobes. The plants grow from 30-90 cm (1-3 ft) tall; the flowers are in terminal clusters on the much-branched plant.

Field Pennycress, *Thlaspi arvense,* has such tiny white flowers the blossoms would be overlooked, but the pods are noticeable and quite attractive. The four small petals are only about one half cm long (.25 in), but the fruit is a flattened, round, penny-shaped pod with a deep notch at the top. There are many such pods on each plant and, as they turn a golden brown, they become attractive. The sessile, toothed leaves are shaped like an arrow, the "ears" at the base seeming to clasp the stem. This plant is common along roads and in pastures, a naturalized European plant. Shepherd's Purse, *Capsella bursa-pastoris,* is somewhat similar, but the pod is smaller and definitely heart-shaped, the basal leaves (in a rosette) resemble those of dandelion.

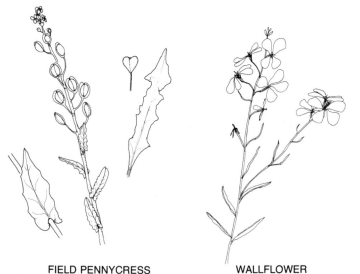

FIELD PENNYCRESS   WALLFLOWER

Wallflower, *Erysimum asperum,* is another European plant which has established itself all over America, though chiefly in the west. It is a beautiful plant with many large yellow-orange fragrant blossoms growing in a crowded raceme. The thick stem has long, narrow, sessile leaves. The European plant was named Wallflower because it is often grew along stone walls, but in America it is found more commonly along roads and in fields in the east or in the mountains of the west.

FIELD MUSTARD

Field Mustard, *Brassica campestris (rapa)*, is a common Mustard with small yellow four-petal flowers growing in a raceme on a branching 30-60 cm tall (12-24 in) plant. The alternate leaves are very characteristic: the upper ones are clasping with ear-like lobes around the stem; they often are irregularly lobed but may be entire. The basal leaves are deeply but irregularly lobed (end lobe much larger), and have a somewhat hairy petiole. The seed pod may be 5-7 cm long (2-3 in) with a slender beak at the tip (as in all *Brassica*). Field Mustard is found throughout the United States.

EVENING PRIMROSE FAMILY
Onagraceae

This is an extremely interesting family. The ovary is inferior, often so far below the flower that it is mistaken for part of the stem. The four sepals are united into a calyx tube which may have a long "neck" above the ovary, the sepal tips bending outwards as the buds open. The four petals are often quite showy in beautiful shades of pink, white, or yellow. There are eight stamens and four stigmas—looking like a plus (+) sign. The members of this family might be mistaken for the Mustard Family, but it is important to remember that Mustards have a superior ovary and six stamens and the members of the Evening Primrose Family have inferior ovaries and eight stamens. Many Evening Primroses (especially the white ones) open late in the afternoon, and are closed by the morning.

Fireweed, *Epilobium augustifolium,* grows all over America from Canada to Florida, west into Texas and Kansas and very widespread in the west, from low valleys to tree line, wherever the soil is moist enough, also in Europe and Asia. It soon covers burned-over areas, and so has earned the common name of Fireweed. It is a tall plant, often growing to two meters (6 ft). The upper third of the stem may be covered with a spike of pinkish-lavender flowers. They have four pinkish sepals joined at the base into a tube, but with four spreading tips. The four pink petals may be 2.5 cm or more wide. Even the drooping buds are colored and showy. The eight purple stamens droop; the style bends downwards until the pollen is dispersed, almost touching the sepal between the two lower petals. As the pollen drops, the style lifts up and the white four-parted stigma opens. The ovary develops into a purplish capsule, and the leaves turn fall colors. Then the capsule opens and air-borne, fluffy seeds are carried by the wind so the plant becomes widely dispersed. The young plants are edible in salads or for greens. The dry leaves were used to make tea.

Sun Drops, *Oenothera fruticosa,* is usually a small, bushy, perennial plant, but may grow to 60 cm (24 in) where conditions are favorable. The bright canary-yellow flowers are 2.5-5 cm (1-2 in) across, the four petals slightly notched. The sepals do not turn back abruptly as with many Evening Primroses. The slender stalk at the base of the ovary is a distinctive characteristic of this species. Four of the eight orange stamens are longer, the long and short stamens alternating. The deep green sessile leaves are pointed at the tips, but variable in shape. Sun Drops can be found from Minnesota and Nova Scotia south to Georgia, blooming from June through August. There are several closely related species, many of them showy in gardens, for they are popular as garden plants and open in the daytime.

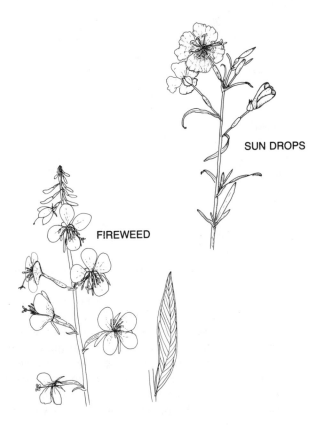

SUN DROPS

FIREWEED

Common Evening Primrose, *Oenothera biennis,* has clear yellow
blossoms 2.5-5 cm (1-2 in) across, often growing as a tall (1-2
meter, 3-6 ft), branched plant from a many-leafed basal rosette.
The stems may become quite red. The calyx tube is much
longer than the stout, ribbed inferior ovary. The flowers grow
from the axils of the long, narrow leaves which alternate up the
hairy stem. This flower can be found across Canada from Newfoundland to Alberta, then south into the northwestern states
and into Texas, and in the east from Maine to Florida; they
grow in dry or sandy fields and along roadsides. It opens in the
evening and often is so abundant in fields it becomes a weed.

COMMON EVENING PRIMROSE

SHOWY EVENING PRIMROSE

Showy Evening Primrose, *Oenothera speciosa,* is a very lovely
flower with large rose or white blossoms, more than 3 cm (1.5
in) across. There are several blossoms and nodding buds on
each slender plant. The seed capsules are strongly 8-ribbed.
The leaves are long and slender, with the flowers growing from
their axils. These flowers are more common in Missouri, Kansas, and Texas, but also are found in the east, often cultivated
and then escaping there. It spreads rapidly and is very hardy.

BUTTERCUP FAMILY
Ranunculaceae

(see family characteristics, Chapter III)

LARKSPUR, *Delphinium*. Most members of the Butter-cup Family have five petals (or no petals), so the family characteristics are described in those chapters, but the general family pattern is a mound of pistils and many stamens. Larkspurs are unusual members, but follow the general pattern. They are more common in the west, but there are about half a dozen species in the east. All species worldwide, including the garden species, resemble one another in shape. They are easy to recognize because of the peculiar shape of the blossom. As the name indicates, the flower has a long spur at the back, which really is one of the five sepals. The sepals are colored like the petals; their color may be purple, blue, violet, white, pink, red, or various shade of these colors, or even multi-colored. There are four petals in unequal pairs, with the upper ones having spurs which are hidden in the long sepal spur. The blossoms grow in a long spike at the tip of each branch. In some species, individual blossoms may be as large as 2 or 3 cm (1+ in) across. Others are smaller, but all are very attractive. Many large-petaled varieties have been developed for gardens.

DWARF LARKSPUR

Dwarf Larkspur, *Delphinium tricorne,* grows from Pennsylvania to Minnesota and south to Georgia, to Oklahoma, flowering from April to June on woody slopes. The spurred flowers are blue or white or variegated. The plants are only about 30 cm (1 ft) tall. The leaves are deeply palmately lobed, resembling buttercup leaves, growing alternately up the slender stalk; upper leaves may be small. These flowers look as if they have five, not four, petals because the sepals are colored like petals and there are five sepals, one with a long spur. The petals are small and curl over the many stamens and the pistils—the flower must be examined to be sure which are sepals and which are petals.

POPPY FAMILY
Papaveraceae

This is a large family, some growing as shrubs. Most Poppies have colored juice, showy flowers, and many stamens. There usually are twice as many petals as sepals, except in Bloodroot and Prickly Poppy (Chapter XI). In some species the sepals are united. All have a compound pistil made up of two or more parts, more or less united. The ovary is superior and is one-celled. The fruit is a capsule with many tiny seeds.

Wood-Poppy, Celandine-Poppy, *Stylophorum diphyllum,* grows mainly in woods of the northeast from Pennsylvania to Virginia and into Tennessee. The four-petalled yellow flower is about 5 cm (2 in) across. The two sepals are hairy. The buds nod, as do the hairy capsules. These flower from March to May on naked stalks. The leaves are opposite and are irregularly and deeply lobed.

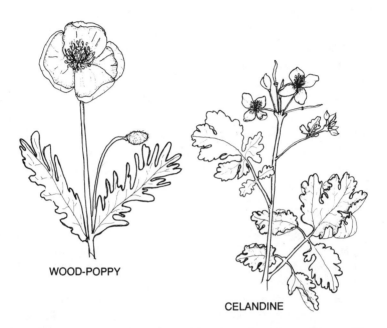

WOOD-POPPY

CELANDINE

Celandine, *Chelidonium majus,* is an introduced weed, very like the Wood-Poppy except the deeply lobed leaves are *alternate,* not opposite. The two sepals fall early, the fragile yellow flowers are small (2.5 cm, 1 in) across and the pistil and seed pod are slender. There are many stamens. This widespread plant grows mainly in moist areas, 30-60 cm tall (12-24 in).

FUMITORY FAMILY
Fumariaceae

The Fumitory Family is closely related to the Poppy Family and some botanists class it as a sub-family (*Fumarioideae*) of the Poppy Family, but the petal shape is very different and is very characteristic. Bleeding Heart belongs to this family. The four petals are in two very different pairs. The outer pair is larger and encloses the inner pair, which is narrower but ridged or crested on the back. One or both of the outer petals is extended backwards into a sac or spur. The inner pair of petals sticks together at the tips and covers the anthers and stigma. The six stamens are in two sets of three each and stand opposite the outer petals; their filaments are united. There are two small, scale-like sepals. The superior ovary is 1-celled and develops into a capsule. The leaves are compound and are very finely dissected— another very distinguishing characteristic. The plants have a colorless, watery sap. There are ten to twelve species of this family in the east. All members are delicate and fern-like and tend to grow in shady, damp areas.

Squirrel Corn, *Dicentra canadensis,* gets its common name from the little corn-like yellow tubers that grow underground. The plant itself looks like California Poppy until it blooms—the blossoms, however, are very different and most unusual! They look like plump white hearts dangling from the arching stem. The four petals are in two pairs, the outer pair enlarged at their base, forming two short, rounded sacs or spurs. There are noticeable crests on the inner petals, the tips of the outer petals spreading apart to reveal the crests and the joined tips of the inner pair. These spring flowers grow to be 30 cm (12 in) tall in woods from Canada to North Carolina, west to Missouri.

SQUIRREL CORN

Dutchman's Breeches, *Dicentra cucullaria,* has white blossoms (sometimes tinged with pink) that actually are shaped like a pair of baggy breeches hanging upside down. The two outer petals of the hanging flower are long-spurred at the base (making the legs of the breeches) and spread open at the yellowish tip to disclose the two narrow inner petals with their tiny yellowish crests. The flowers grow in nodding clusters and are quite fragrant. The plant is much like Squirrel Corn, with fern-like, much divided bluish-green leaves. This plant is *poisonous* to animals. It grows all over the east in woods, as far west as Arkansas and from Nova Scotia west to eastern Oregon and Washington.

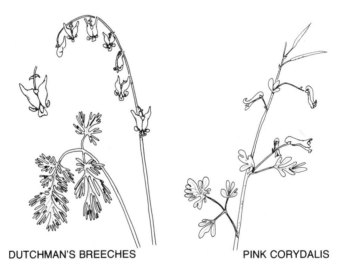

DUTCHMAN'S BREECHES   PINK CORYDALIS

Pink or Pale Corydalis, *Corydalis sempervirens,* grows from Canada to Georgia and Tennessee, on rocky ledges and in woods. The leaves have a whitish bloom, and are not quite so fern-like and finely divided as the above two plants, but it, too, is delicate. The pale pink flowers are about 2 cm long (less than 1 in), with two small sepals and only one of the outer pair of petals elongated backward into a spur. The turned-back tips are yellowish. Other close relatives have yellow flowers. Yellow Fumewort, *Corydalis flavula,* has crested tips on the outer petals and grows from Connecticut to Kansas.

Chapter VI

FLOWERS WITH FOUR UNITED PETALS

Some flowers in this chapter have their petals united only near the base; others, like Gentian, are united except for the tips, and so are deeply tubular. Some Gentians, of course, will also be found in a later chapter, for some species have five united petals. Many flowers with four united petals have petals all the same shape, but in Veronicas (Speedwells), the lower petal is smaller and often lighter-colored.

MADDER FAMILY
Rubiaceae

Some members of this family are herbs and some are shrubs. The leaves are opposite, or whorled. There are four sepals, four united petals, four stamens, and a two-celled inferior ovary. The sepals are fused to the ovary. Many have tiny flowers. Coffee is a member of this family.

Bluets, Innocense, Quaker Ladies, *Houstonia caerulea,* is a low, tufted or matted plant which grows in masses all over the east from Nova Scotia and Ontario to Wisconsin, south to Georgia, Alabama, and Missouri. Often it grows in such abundance that it looks like drifts of snow with a pale blue cast. The 1 cm wide flowers are unusually dainty, a lovely shade of blue, lavender, white, or occasionally pink, with a yellowish-white center. The petals are joined into a basal tube, but with the tips spread out at right angles into four lobes. The ovary is inferior, with the sepals growing about halfway up around the ovary. The stem leaves are opposite, the basal leaves form a rosette.

Northern Bedstraw, *Galium boreale,* has very tiny fragrant white flowers in tight clusters. The four (sometimes three) petals are joined at the base into a tiny tube. There are four (sometimes three) stamens, two styles, and the inferior ovary matures into two small, round, dry fruits. The stem is squarish and almost vine-like or sprawling, up to a meter in length. The leaves grow in whorls of four, and the whole plant is more or less hairy. This plant grows in open woods from Canada to Alaska, south to Delaware, west to Missouri, and in the western states. Also found across Europe and Asia—a circumpolar plant.

Partridge Berry, *Mitchella repens,* has small, shiny, evergreen leaves in pairs. The little waxy, white, fragrant flowers are also in pairs, with bases touching. One of the flower pair has four long stamens and a short style and the other of the pair has four short stamens and a long style. The stamens are attached to the hairy throat of the tube, with the anthers protruding. One *united* fruit develops from the two flowers. It looks very much like a tiny cherry and persists through the winter. They are edible but not meaty. Found in woods from Newfoundland to Minnesota, south to Florida and Texas.

NORTHERN BEDSTRAW

BLUETS

PARTRIDGE BERRY

GENTIAN FAMILY
Gentianaceae

The Gentians are a family of lovely wildflowers with color-less, bitter juice. They appear in this chapter and in Chapter IX because some species have four united petals and others have five united petals. Whichever number of petals they have, the other flower parts follow that plan. Generally the petals are united into a distinct funnel or tube, often fringed at the tip, but the petals may be united only near the base. They tend to be spirally twisted in the bud. The leaves are sessile, either opposite or whorled. Both sepals and petals tend to dry persistent. Stamens are of the same number as petal lobes, attached to the throat or tube of the corolla. The superior ovary is one-celled, the fruit a capsule. There are about four hundred different species in the United States, many of them in the east.

Fringed Gentian, *Gentiana crinita,* has four bright blue (some-times white) united petals, the fringed lobes swirling out from the vase-like corolla tube. The flowers close at night. The four stamens are attached to the base of the petal tube and can be seen only by looking deep into the flower. It grows 30-90 cm (1-3 ft) tall, with oval, pointed, opposite leaves on somewhat angled stems. Fringed Gentian grows in moist meadows and woods from Canada to Georgia, west to Minnesota, a lovely wildflower to find.

FRINGED GENTIAN

FIGWORT FAMILY
Scrophularaceae

(see Chapter X for family write-up)

Speedwells or Veronicas are unusual "scrophs" in that they only have four petal lobes, the upper one usually the largest, but the lowest one definitely smaller or narrower, the side ones quite round. The flowers are fairly small, and are usually blue, striped in darker blue; sometimes they are white or the bottom lobe is white. They only have two stamens. The ovary develops into a heart-shaped capsule. There are about twenty species in the east, all low, creeping plants, frequently with just one small flower in each upper leaf axil, or flowers may be in slender racemes from the leaf axis. Some are natives, some came from Europe where they are very common.

Veronica persica, is a creeping plant with hairy stems and coarsely toothed leaves. The flowers are single in the leaf axils. The petal lobes are bright blue, marked with dark blue lines, the flower light in the center and about 1 cm across. The seed capsule is a small, broad, squat, heart-shape with rather pointed lobes, the persistent calyx very hairy. This Speedwell is widely spread, blooming from March to September from Newfoundland to Alaska, south to Florida, west to Indiana, and in the Pacific states.

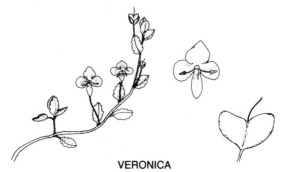

VERONICA

Chapter VII

FIVE SEPARATE PETALS ALL ALIKE

Most of the flowers of the world have five petals, including a number of trees and shrubs, but there are many variations. This chapter contains just the flowers with five separate petals all alike. Chapter VIII has flowers with five separate petals, but the petals are not all the same shape. Flowers with five united petals, all the petal lobes being the same shape, will be in Chapter IX. Irregular flowers, those appearing two-lipped because the lobes of the united petals are not all the same shape, will be found in Chapter X.

ROSE FAMILY
Rosaceae

This is a very large family with much variety and consists of herbs, vines, shrubs, and trees. Many of our garden flowers and fruit trees belong to this family: roses, apples, pears, and berries are a few that are very useful to man. In spite of all the variety, members of this family can be recognized because the leaves are alternate, often compound, with stipules. The calyx is five-parted, in some appearing to be ten-parted because of a row of bracts attached just below the calyx. The five separate petals may be pink, red, yellow, or white. There may be only five stamens, but usually there are many, and are attached to the calyx or to a disc that lines the calyx tube. The few to many ovaries may be joined to form a compound pistil with one to many styles or stigmas. The fruits may be achenes, berries, pods, or pomes. The Rose Family has about 3200 species, many of which are native Americans.

Wild Rose, *Rosa*. There are about twenty-four species of wild roses in the eastern United States, all much alike. *Rosa carolina* is a low-growing species in dry open woods or slopes from Maine to Florida. *Rosa setigera* is a shrubby rose which trails along roadsides from New York to Florida, west to Texas. *Rosa palustris* is a strong erect plant which grows in swamps and in damp woods from Canada to Florida, west to Arkansas. *Rosa laevigata* is a high-climbing species found throughout the east. All species look much alike, although some are pink, some white, some yellow, but they are easy to recognize as Wild Roses with their five separate petals and many stamens attached to the calyx or the rim.

WILD ROSE   WILD STRAWBERRY

Wild Strawberry, *Fragaria virginiana,* looks much like a garden strawberry. It spreads by runners from which grow compound leaves with three leaflets each. The flowering stems are 10-30 cm (4-12 in) tall, with many small white blossoms with five white petals and five sepals. Red, sweet berries develop from the ovaries of the blossoms. These little plants spread in solid mats along roads and trails, in meadows, and along streams all over the east.

FLOWERING RASPBERRY

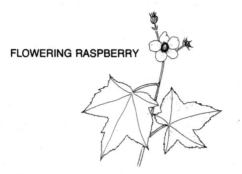

Flowering Raspberry, *Rubus odoratus,* has clusters of deep pink, rose-like blossoms 2.5-5 cm (1-2 in) across. The plant is large enough to be considered a shrub, with semi-woody canes which are bristly but thornless. The leaves are large and maple-like (but not shiny), pubescent on the veins underneath. It grows in woods and thickets from Canada south to Georgia, west to Michigan. The fruit is a dry and acid berry.

Blackberry, *Rubus frondosus,* grows in almost every woodsy place from New England to Virginia, west to Indiana. Whole fence rows can be white with its lovely little blossoms. The plants are vine-like, thorny, and become a tangled mass that is a great nuisance. The flowers are borne on spineless stems with many blossoms, each developing into a juicy, delicious berry.

BLACKBERRY

Cinquefoil, Five-Finger, *Potentilla.* There are many species in
this genus, all so much alike that only small botanical differ-
ences distinguish many of them. However, all have five petals,
usually yellow (a few have white petals), many stamens, and
many small pistils. Below the petals are five sepals and below
them, usually smaller, and alternating with them, are five bracts
which seem like additional sepals. These characteristics are
similar to Buttercups, but Buttercups do not have bracts, so
this is one distinguishing characteristic. Also, in the Rose Family the stamens are attached to a disc that lines the calyx. The
word "Cinquefoil" means five leaves, for this plant has five
leaflets in its compound leaf. Many of the Cinquefoils have
palmately compound leaves, but some are pinnately compound. Some species are small creeping plants looking much
like a strawberry with yellow blossoms. Others are plants 30-60
cm (1-2 ft) tall. Cinquefoils can be found all over the east. A
common one is *Potentilla canadensis,* the Dwarf Cinquefoil
found in dry meadows with very silvery gray stems and leaflets
with teeth only from the tip to midway. It spreads by runners.

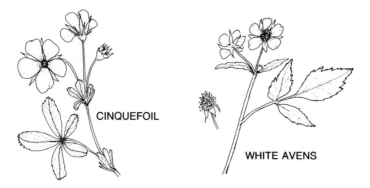

CINQUEFOIL

WHITE AVENS

White Avens, *Geum canadense.* Most of this genus of plants
have pinnately compound leaves, with the end leaflet larger
than those at the sides, the upper leaves simple. This plant is
slender, with several blossoms at tips of branches. The five
white petals are spaced far apart, with the five green sepals
showing between. The many stamens surround the green pistils, making a bright little flower. The seed pod is bristly. Found
from Minnesota to Nova Scotia south.

GERANIUM FAMILY
Geraniaceae

Geraniums are well known throughout most of the world. There is some variation in the kinds of leaves, but the blossoms and fruit are quite characteristic. They all have seed pods which are long and slender, developing rapidly after the petals fall. Five seeds develop in the five-parted ovary, each remaining connected to its style, forming the characteristic long seed pod. When ripe, the five parts separate, each style stays attached to one seed and twists as a corkscrew tail, helping to separate it from the others, and to twist its seed down into the ground. There are five sepals, five petals, and five or ten stamens.

Cranesbill, *Erodium maculatum,* is the commonest species of large wild geranium. The flower is a beautiful rose-pink, about 2-3 cm (1+ in) across. The leaves are palmately lobed into five hairy parts, each lobe serrate. The loveliest blossoms are in groups of three or more, growing in woods on plants about 60 cm (24 in) tall. The long, slender seedpod (shaped like a bird's beak, hence the name) is very noticeable and characteristic.

CRANESBILL

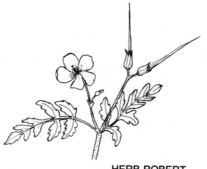

HERB ROBERT

Herb Robert, *Geranium robertianum,* looks much like Cranes-bill, except the blossoms are not so large (1-2 cm, ½ in), and are usually just in pairs. Also the leaves are more finely divided, and are pinnately (not palmately) divided into three or five serrated sections, the larger end lobe on a long stalk. The reddish stem is noticeably hairy. Herb Robert, too, develops the long characteristic seed pod (beak) of this family.

PINK FAMILY
Caryophyllaceae

Members of the Pink Family have five separate petals that are usually notched or cleft at the tip. The sepals may be separate or united (as in *Silene*). When united, they often form a swollen "vase" around the petals; commonly they are the conspicuous part of the flower. Generally there are five sepals, sometimes only four. Pinks usually have swollen joints on the stems, called nodes. The leaves are opposite and simple. Pinks must not be confused with the Phlox Family that have five *united* petals; many Pinks form mats of color, as do the Phlox, so it is important to examine the petals. The stamens are the same number, or double the number, as the petals. Garden pinks include the Carnations. Often they are fragrant.

Wild Pink, *Silene carolina,* grows as a lowish clump with pink
blossoms about 2.5 cm (1 in) across in loose clusters on hairy
stems. The petals are wedge-shaped with slightly toothed tips.
The five sticky, united sepals are joined into a tube; there are
ten stamens, and the fruit is a small capsule, the sepals enlarg-
ing around it. The perennial plant produces a thick tuft of narrow basal leaves; leaves may grow up to 10 cm long (4 in),
wider near the tip. The opposite stem leaves are much smaller.
This pink grows from New England to Georgia, mainly in the
mountains in dry or sandy soils.

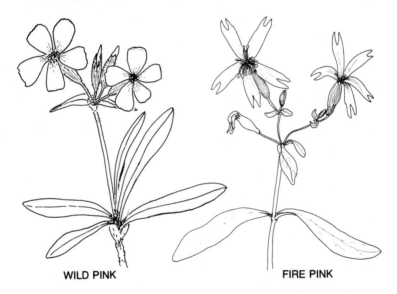

WILD PINK   FIRE PINK

Fire Pink, *Silene virginica,* makes masses of brilliant color along
roadsides, the flowers growing in open clusters. Each flower is
2-3 cm or more across (1+ in), and a vibrant bright red. Each
petal is notched into two deep lobes. The sepals are united into
a long tube with five tips. The opposite leaves are pointed, with
several pairs along the stem, and growing to be many centimeters long—up to 30 cm (12 in). They are widest above the
middle. Fire Pinks grow in open woods and on sandy hillsides
from western New York and Ontario into the southeastern
states. Very lovely ones can be found in the Great Smoky
Mountains, blooming all summer.

Bladder Campion, *Silene cucubalus,* is a European plant which
has become a roadside weed from New England to Virginia,
west to Missouri—in fact, over much of North America. The
pale tannish-pink united sepals form the noticeable part of the
flowers. They form a large, urn-shaped, noticeably veined and
ribbed puffy container for the five deeply notched small white
petals, this "bladder" growing larger as the flower fades. The
flowers are somewhat nodding. They grow in a loose raceme
with many flowers on each plant. The pointed leaves are opposite.

BLADDER CAMPION   STARRY CAMPION

Starry Campion, *Silene stellata,* has five very fringed white petals
which sit in a large vase formed by the united sepals. The plant
grows to about one meter (3 ft), with stiff, slender stems. The
blossoms are borne in a loose raceme at the top. The pointed
leaves are in whorls around the stem, usually with four leaves
at a node, downy on the undersurface. Starry Campion can be
found in woods from New England to Georgia and west to
North Dakota.

Bouncing Bet or Soapwort, *Saponaria officialis,* is another European plant which has become a common weed throughout the east and midwest, growing in great clumps along roads and in fields. Its pale pinkish, fragrant flowers are borne in close clusters on meter-tall (3 ft) plants. The notched petals tend to reflex somewhat, producing a characteristic flower cluster. The opposite, oval, pointed leaves have three main veins. Flowers low on the stem usually grow in the axis of each leaf (so they tend to be in pairs), or in groups of four—sometimes more, near the stem tip. The sap forms a soapy lather, but is *poisonous.* This plant blooms all summer.

BOUNCING BET   STAR CHICKWEED

Star Chickweed, *Stellaria pubera.* Many chickweeds are small, prostrate plants, often found in lawns. Star Chickweed is slender but taller, with star-like white flowers with very deeply notched petals (almost appearing like ten petals), growing in clusters, surrounded by wide sepals which are just barely shorter than the petals. The plants are about 30 cm (24 in) tall, with opposite, mostly sessile leaves up to 7 cm long (2.5 in), and angled stems. A woodsy plant from New Jersey to Alabama, west to Illinois, flowering all spring.

MALLOW FAMILY
Malvaceae

This large family is found over much of the world. The most easily recognized characteristic is the collar or column of many stamens with at least the base of their filaments united, surrounding the compound pistil. The claws of the five separate petals are united to the base of this column. There are five sepals united at the base, but often there is a row of bracts below them, so it looks as though there are ten sepals. The five petals may twist in the bud. The mature ovary in many species looks like a flat cheese, giving the common name of "cheese weed" to some members. The ovary splits apart into kidney-shaped sections (like an orange). Most Mallows have perfect flowers, but some have separate staminate and pistillate flowers, some have staminate and pistillate plants. All have a sticky, stringy juice. The leaves are alternate, simple, palmately veined and lobed, and often very beautiful. Both leaves and stems may be hairy. Many have very beautiful flowers. Hollyhocks and Hibiscus are favorite garden Mallows. Marshmallows, in the early days, were made from the sticky juices of a mallow that grew in the marshes. Cotton and Okra are important commercial members of this family.

Swamp Rose Mallow, *Hibiscus moscheutos,* is an unusually beautiful mallow, with blooms as much as 20 cm (8 in) across, growing on a two meter (6 ft) plant. The petals are white to cream, with crimson bases. Masses of these lovely flowers grow in marshes all over the east, west to Indiana, making a spectacular sight. This species is very similar to *Hibiscus palustris* which has bigger, often pink or purplish flowers and wider leaves.

Musk Mallow, *Malva moschata,* grows from New England to Maryland and west to Nebraska, a European plant which has established itself here. It is a smaller plant than the Swamp Rose Mallow—usually only to 60 cm (24 in). Its leaves are deeply lobed into narrow segments. Its pink, veined blossoms are about 5 cm (2 in) across, the notched petals with crinkled edges, and the characteristic column of united stamens. There are three bracts below the sepals.

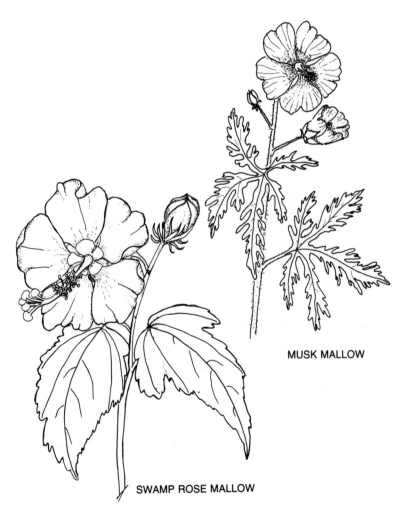

MUSK MALLOW

SWAMP ROSE MALLOW

BUTTERCUP FAMILY
Ranunculaceae

(family characteristics in Chapter III)

Tall or Meadow Buttercup, *Ranunculus acris,* is a common but lovely wildflower all summer, widespread in the east from Canada to Virginia, west to Oklahoma. It grows to one meter (3 ft) or more, with branching stems. The flowers are waxy yellow to white, all very glossy. There is a small nectar gland near the base of each of the five petals. There are five green sepals, many stamens and many pistils. Each pistil forms a small achene, so the seed head is made of many pieces. The alternate leaves are palmately divided.

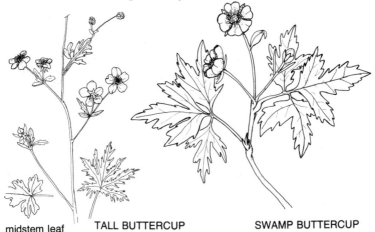

midstem leaf   TALL BUTTERCUP   SWAMP BUTTERCUP

Swamp Buttercup, *Ranunculus septentrionalis,* has bright yellow flowers much like the Tall Buttercup, but they are larger, growing more than 3 cm (1+ in) across. The plants are 30-90 cm (1-3 ft) tall with smooth, hollow stems which may trail along the ground, rooting at the nodes. The long-stemmed large leaves have three main divisions, each deeply cleft (and each lobe is also stemmed). Sometimes the lower leaves may have petioles 30 cm (12 in) long. This Buttercup grows in swamps, marshes, and damp fields from Canada to Georgia, west to Kansas, flowering from April through July.

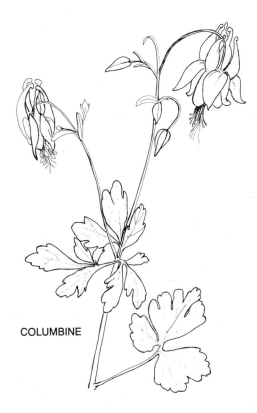

COLUMBINE

Columbine, *Aquilegia canadensis,* is one of the loveliest wildflowers, with its colorful and graceful nodding flowers. The five colored sepals are petal-like and usually stand out backwards. The five bright petals have long hollow spurs extending behind the calyx. The leaves are compound and each leaflet has two or three lobes or divisions, making a dainty, almost fern-like plant. There are many stamens and five separate simple pistils which develop into a head of five separate many-seeded pods. Columbines grow on rocky ledges and in woods all over the United States. The sepals are red and the spurs on the petals also are red, but the tips of the petals are yellow. The long yellow stamens hang down below the nodding flowers.

PITCHER PLANT FAMILY
Sarraceniaceae

The strange plants that belong to this family have peculiar pitcher-shaped leaves, which give them their common name. These form a basal rosette. All are hollow, and the insides are densely covered with stiff, downward-pointing hairs. There is a wing-like ridge up the outside. Each leaf produces an enticing nectar which is attractive to insects. When an unsuspecting creature enters, it goes down easily, but cannot get back up because of the stiff hairs. Rain water also is trapped inside the pitcher, so the insect drowns in it. The flowers are unusual, too. They are solitary, each hanging head downward from a leafless stem. They have three bracts, five sepals, five petals, and many stamens. The pistil has a style shaped something like an open umbrella, with a stigma under each point of the umbrella.

Pitcher Plant, or Flytrap, *Sarracenia purpurea,* looks something like a pitcher half lying down on the ground, but twisted so its open mouth points upward. These are the greenish-yellow or purplish, heavily veined persistent leaves of the plant. The flowers are deep red and follow the family pattern of five greenish or colored sepals (which persist), five deep crimson (or pink) petals that curve inwards and soon fall off, many stamens and the broad, petal-like umbrella-shaped stigma. The naked flowering stalk is 30-46 cm (12-18 in) tall. These plants grow in swampy areas from Canada west to the Rockies, south to Florida and to the Mississippi Valley, more common in the northern parts of this area.

Trumpets, *Sarracenia flava,* has long, tube-like hollow leaves with a "flap" or hood which curves over the opening. The ridge is not large as in *S. purpurea.* These leaves are yellow, or greenish-yellow. The bright yellow flowers have long, narrow petals extending beyond the big pistil. Trumpets grow in bogs in pine lands, often in large clumps, from Virginia to Florida and Alabama.

PITCHER PLANT

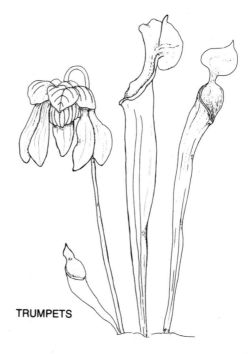

TRUMPETS

OXALIS FAMILY
Oxalidaceae

These small plants have sour juice and palmately compound leaves with three heart-shaped leaflets (appearing somewhat like clover leaves). The leaves can be used in salads to give a tangy flavor. The juice is sour, which gives the common name of "sour clover." The leaves often fold and droop at night. The flowers may be white, pink, lavender or bright yellow, often veined. They are built on the plan of five, with five sepals, five petals, and ten stamens, which usually are in two rows of five each, with their filaments united at the base. There are five styles and the superior five-celled ovary develops into a many-seeded capsule. Many of the family grow in the tropics, but several species are common in the east. Some species just have leaves from the base, others have leaves on the stems.

Common Wood-Sorrel, *Oxalis montana,* grows 5-15 cm (2-6 in) tall, the flowers solitary on their stalks, the leaves all from the base. The white or pink petals are notched, and veined with pink or purple, the color heavier in a "ring" around the center. These pretty wood flowers may be 2-3 cm (1 in) across, growing from Canada to North Carolina.

COMMON WOOD-SORREL   VIOLET WOOD-SORREL

Violet Wood-Sorrel, *Oxalis violacea*, gets its name not only from its pinkish-violet colored flowers but also because the underside of the leaves is violet or crimson. It grows 10-20 cm (4-8 in) tall, the blossoms standing above the basal leaves. There are several flowers on the leafless flowering stalk, the petals quite broad. This Oxalis grows in open woods from New England to Florida to New Mexico, flowering from April to July.

Creeping Sorrel, *Oxalis repens* (also called *Oxalis corniculata* by some). This common weed from Europe is all over America. It is a tiny sorrel of fields, roadsides, lawns, and nurseries, with leafy, weak, creeping stems, which may root at the nodes. The stems and leaves may be tinged with purple or bronze and have dark brown stipules. The small flowers are yellow, growing singly on their stalk but scattered along the creeping stem. They are often less than 1 cm across. The seeds are in an upright angled capsule.

Large Yellow Wood-Sorrel, *Oxalis grandis*, as the name implies is a big yellow Sorrel, with blossoms 2.5 cm (1 in) across, the leaves up to 5 cm (2 in) across, and with hairy stems a meter or more tall (3+ ft). The flowers grow in clusters, just showing above the leaves. Often the leaves are purplish along the edges. It, too, is a Wood-Sorrel, found mainly from Pennsylvania west to Illinois, and south to Georgia and Alabama.

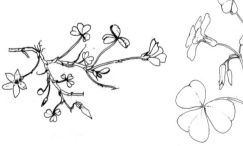

CREEPING SORREL   LARGE YELLOW WOOD SORREL

PURSLANE FAMILY
Portulacaceae

Many members of this family grow in the west, but there are two very welcome ones in the east which announce the arrival of spring. This is a family of low plants, many with weak stems. The opposite leaves usually are succulent-thick and juicy. Generally the showy flowers have an unusual pattern of two sepals with five petals (Bitterroot, the state flower of Montana, has many petals). The stamen number may vary from five to many. The fruit is a capsule with two or three sections. The flowers tend to be very fragile, opening only in sunlight and soon withering. The Portulaca (Moss Rose) in gardens is a member of this family.

Virginia Spring Beauty, *Claytonia virginica*, grows in thick, sprawling masses in moist woods, blooming early in the spring. They are lovely, dainty little flowers of soft pink or white, striped with dark pink. When picked, the flowers close tightly; they also close if the sun is not shining. The stems grow 10-30 cm (4-12 in) tall from deep perennial roots. The paired leaves midway up the stem are shiny and grass-like, an identifying characteristic for Spring Beauty. The many flowers grow in loose clusters. Each flower is 1-2.5 cm (.5-1 in) across, the five stamens attached to the base of the petals, the anthers pink. They grow from eastern Canada to Montana and south to North Carolina and Texas.

Carolina Spring Beauty, *Claytonia caroliniana*, has flowers very much like those of Virginia Spring Beauty, except they may be a little smaller, have fewer flowers on the stalk, and often are white with pink veins (but may be pink). The paired leaves, however, are the distinguishing characteristic, because the Carolina Spring Beauty has quite wide, paired stem leaves, growing on short petioles. These grow from Canada to North Carolina, west to Missouri mainly in the mountains, rarely near the coast.

VIRGINIA SPRING BEAUTY

CAROLINA SPRING BEAUTY

SAXIFRAGE FAMILY
Saxifragaceae

The wildflowers in this family usually have small blossoms (often very intricate and interesting), with beautiful, mostly basal leaves. The flowers are generally on tall, slender flower stalks. The flower structure is very like the Rose Family, with five sepals and five petals, though usually there are only five (or ten) stamens, attached to the calyx edge. The styles and stigmas are separate and not as numerous as the petals. The two ovaries are lightly joined only at the base and vary in position from wholly inferior to superior, developing into a capsule or berry. The wild species mostly grow on rocky ledges and streambanks. Coral Bells are common garden plants, and currants and gooseberries also belong to this family.

Foam Flower or False Miterwort, *Tiarella cordifolia*, makes masses of fluffy, creamy-white flowers growing on slender stalks about 30 cm (1 ft) high. The tiny flowers grow in a tight raceme. They have five tiny petals, five white sepals and ten orange or reddish stamens, making the flower very airy-appearing. The leaves are all basal, shaped like maple leaves. They are covered with fine hairs on their upper sides. Sometimes they are mottled with brown. This grows from Canada to North Carolina and west to Tennessee.

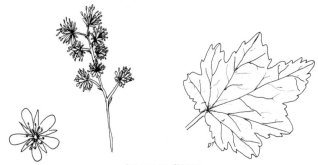

FOAM FLOWER

Bishop's Cap or Miterwort, *Mitella diphylla*, gets its common name from the two-beaked flower capsule which looks something like a bishop's cap. The tiny flowers grow in a narrow raceme. Each flower has five finely fringed petals, the flower looking like a tiny snowflake under a magnifying glass. Halfway up the hairy flowering stalk are two opposite sessile leaves (hence the species name). The rough-hairy basal leaves are dark green, and are deeply lobed at the base. They have a slightly lobed margin, and are on long petioles. They are similar to maple leaves in shape. Clumps of these are found all over New England, each producing several flowering stalks.

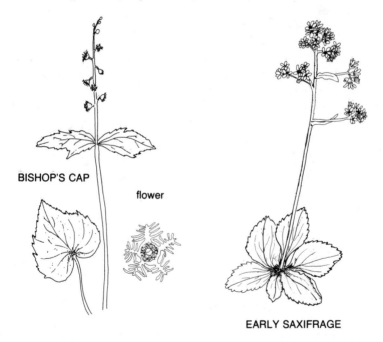

BISHOP'S CAP

flower

EARLY SAXIFRAGE

Early Saxifrage, *Saxifraga virginiensis*, grows on rocky hillsides from Canada to Georgia to Missouri, flowering from April to June. At flowering time it is only about 10 cm (4 in) tall, but later the sticky-hairy stem elongates to about 40 cm (18 in). The leaves are all basal and hairy. The five-petaled white or greenish flowers are very small, growing in clusters. The ten stamens are bright yellow and protrude beyond the petals.

Grass-of-Parnassus, *Parnassia glauca*, is totally ungrass-like. The flowers grow on tall stalks 30 cm (12 in) or longer from long-petioled, spade-like, basal leaves. The leaf veinage is very characteristic, extending from the base, unbranched, to the tip. Each flower stalk has a clasping leaf about midway. The flower fits the family pattern of five separate sepals, five petals, each strongly veined with yellow or green. These flowers, however, have short sepals and broad petals. There are five fertile stamens which alternate with the petals, plus staminoidea, usually in groups of three, standing in front of the petals, making the center of the flower very interesting. The fruit is a capsule. This species grows in swampy meadows from New England to Pennsylvania, flowering all summer and fall. *P. palustris* is another northeastern species with very round bladed leaves deeply indented at the base and hair-like staminoidea. There are several other very similar species in the southeast, such as *P. caroliniana* with roundish leaves, *P. asarifolia* with broad leaves, and *P. grandifolia* with very long staminoidea. Grass-of-Parnassus is one of the largest flowering members of the Saxifrage Family.

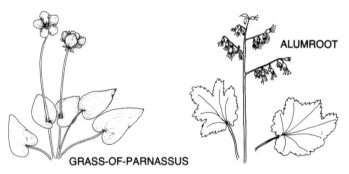

ALUMROOT

GRASS-OF-PARNASSUS

Alumroot, *Heuchera americana*, is a variable species, with tall flowering stalks, the tiny flowers hanging from short stems in a loose raceme. They are greenish-yellow or reddish with tiny petals. The five stamens extend beyond the tiny petals and their orange anthers are the most noticeable part. The basal leaves are lobed and toothed. Alumroot is wide spread, growing in dry rocky woods from New England to Michigan, south to Georgia and Oklahoma.

ST. JOHN'S-WORT FAMILY
Hypericaceae

The flowers in this family have five petals (sometimes four), five (or four) separate sepals, the numerous stamens joined at their bases into bunches. The pistil usually has five styles and the ovary is usually divided into five sections. Translucent glands on the leaves make them look as though there are holes in them. In some species the petals are spotted with black glands. Most of the eastern members of the family are herbs but some are shrubs. The flowers of all are similiar. The leaves are opposite, usually sessile.

Tall St. John's-Wort, *Hypericum pyramidatum*, may be almost two meters (6 ft) tall. The bright yellow, showy flowers are 2.5-5 cm (1-2 in) across, growing in a loose terminal cluster. There are five pointed sepals, five rounded petals, and the very numerous stamens are arranged in five bunches. The five styles are united at the base, the fruit an oval pod. The opposite, elliptic leaves are large. This plant makes bright spots along streams from Canada to Pennsylvania and west to Iowa and Minnesota. It blooms all summer.

TALL ST. JOHN'S WORT

COMMON ST. JOHN'S-WORT

Common St. John's-Wort, *Hypericum perforatum*, is a much-branched plant usually less than a meter (3 ft) tall. The bright yellow flowers are borne in clusters on the tips of the many branches. They are about 2.5 cm (1 in) across, the five petals having black dots along the edges. The many stamens are united at their base into three sets, not five. There are three styles, and the fruit is an oval pod. The opposite leaves are sessile and are also black dotted. This European plant has become a common roadside weed over much of America.

PARSLEY or CARROT FAMILY
Umbelliferae

The *Umbelliferae* Family was given its name because the tiny flowers are arranged in umbels; "umbrella" comes from the same Latin word. Often there are umbels within the main umbel, making a very big lacy arrangement. The umbel is usually surrounded by petal-like bracts (together they are called an involucre), some of them quite large. Most members have white or whitish flowers, but some are yellow. The flowers of all the family are so much alike that the different groups are identified mainly by the fruit, which is dry and seed-like. The tiny flowers have five sepals, five petals, five stamens and an inferior ovary with two styles. The fruit is in two halves, the seeds face to face, their backs having various ribs, wings, prickles, hairs, and oil tube arrangements. The small oil tubes make many of them strong-smelling. The stems of most are hollow; some of them grow very tall, up to two and a half meters (8 ft). The leaves are alternate or basal, and usually finely divided, often compound. The umbels dry persistent, and may be used for winter decoration. Many plants of the family have been used since ancient times as food or seasoning, such as roots of carrot and parsnips, leaves or stems of parsley and celery, seeds of anise and caraway. Some members are *very poisonous* to both grazing animals and humans; some are useful in medicine. However, there are so many poisonous species that *no wild member of this family should be eaten unless the identification is positive.*

Queen Anne's Lace, Wild Carrot, Bird's Nest, *Daucus carota*, is a common weed of fields and roadsides. The three-forked bracts (involucre) below the umbel is characteristic. It is a European plant which has become a nuisance in pastures and fields. The tiny flowers are white (or creamy or pinkish) and grow so closely together that they form a flat lacy mass. In the center of each umbel there often is a single small, dark red or purple flower. As the flowers wither, the whole compound umbel curls up and inward, the deep head resembling an untidy bird's nest. The plants usually stand 60-100 cm (2-3 ft) tall with bristly stems and fern-like pinnately compound leaves. It is a near relative of the garden carrot.

QUEEN ANNE'S LACE

Spotted Cowbane or Water-Hemlock, *Cicuta maculata*. Spotted Cowbane is a smooth, stout, branching plant one or two meters tall growing in damp areas. This is an extremely *poisonous* plant, any part of it—a small piece can kill even a cow in a few minutes. The blossoms are compound umbels—each about 10 cm (4 in) across. They are made up of many tiny white flowers whose petals curve inward. The stout stems are streaked with purple and bear many large pinnately compound leaves; sometimes the nine to twenty-one leaflets again divide. The sharply toothed leaflets are narrow, the veins run to the notches between the teeth. The lower leaves may be 30 cm (12 in) long. Water-Hemlock grows from Canada to Florida, west to Texas and the Dakotas, flowering all summer along streams, in wet meadows, and fields.

Water-Parsnip, *Sium suave*, is big and has flowers very much like Spotted Cowbane, but the stems are not spotted; instead they are ridged like corrugated cardboard. The pinnately compound leaves have three to seven pairs of narrow, toothed leaflets. If standing in water the lower leaves may be even more finely divided. This species grows from 60-180 cm (2-6 ft) tall in marshes all over the country from Nova Scotia to Florida, west to British Columbia and California.

Alexanders, *Zizia trifoliata*, produces masses of golden flowers in compound umbels with no bracts. The little blossoms have incurving petals, the central flower of each umbel having no stalk. The stem and basal leaves are alike—divided into threes and then redivided into threes, with toothed margins. The plants are 30-100 cm (1-3 ft) tall. They grow in damp woods, mainly in the mountain areas of the southeast—Virginia, Kentucky, and Tennessee.

Golden Alexanders, *Zizia aurea*, is perhaps more common over the whole east than Alexanders. Golden Alexanders can be found in damp woods and meadows from Canada to Georgia and Texas blooming in late spring and into summer. It is very like *Z. trifoliata* except the leaf margins are only serrate, not deeply toothed.

SPOTTED COWBANE

× ⅛

basal leaf

WATER PARSNIP

× ⅛

ALEXANDERS

× ½

HEATH FAMILY
(including *Pyrolaceae*)
Ericaceae

This is a large family with much variety, which now includes the Wintergreen Family (*Pyrolaceae*) which once was classified as a separate family. The Heaths include such shrubs as Azalea, Rhododendron, Laurel, and Blueberry. Most of the eastern members are shrubs, but some are herbs, generally found in woods or in the mountains. The flowers have five (rarely four) petals and sepals. The petals may be separate, partly united, or completely united into vase-shaped flowers (Heathers). The ones in this chapter have separate petals. The lower petal in some is somewhat larger and more highly colored. Flowers may be red, pink, or white. They have five to ten stamens. The calyx is persistent, the ovary is usually five-celled and superior with a long, persistent style. The fruit may be a berry, but most Heaths produce a capsule with a hard outer surface. This capsule, split into five parts, often persists, standing or hanging from its stem through the winter. Some members of this family have no green parts, and so cannot make their own food. They are saprophytes whose roots grow in close association with fungus which breaks down forest humus into a form that saprophytes can use.

Indian-pipe, *Monotropa uniflora*, is an amazing plant, for it lacks chlorophyll and lives as a saprophyte in rich woodlands. It is waxy-white or pinkish in color, ghost-like in the woods, but becomes blackish as it dries up. Several stalks grow from a mass of roots. A single flower droops at the top of each 5-30 cm (2-12 in) thick translucent stem. There are five oblong petals, the sepals scale-like, and the large ovary becomes tannish and stands upright as it matures. There are no leaves, just thin scale-like bracts along the stem. It grows nearly everywhere in Canada and the United States where there are deep woods.

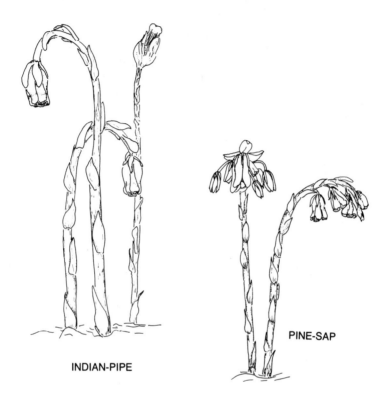

PINE-SAP

INDIAN-PIPE

Pine-sap, *Monotropa hypopithys*, is another saprophyte in this family. It is similar to Indian-pipe but several little flowers droop from the tip of the 25-35 cm (10-14 in) stem. It is yellowish, tannish, or reddish and has a fragrance. The five petals are fine-hairy both inside and out. This grows from Canada to Mexico in moist woods where leaf mold is deep.

Shinleaf, Wintergreen, *Pyrola rotundifolia*, is a low-growing evergreen plant with white veins or spots in its thick, shiny, round or oval basal leaves. The basal leaves often have very long petioles. The leafless flowering stalk has ten to twenty small hanging, white or greenish open bell-shaped flowers. The lowest petal is somewhat larger than the other four. The ten stamens turn toward the upper petals. The long style bends down towards the largest petal, and then turns outwards. The five petals are rounded and spreading. Wintergreen grows from New England to Georgia, west to Michigan, blooming all summer. Another Shinleaf is *Pyrola elliptica*, a smaller plant with basal leaves elliptical (but rounded at the tip), and the blade is longer than the petiole.

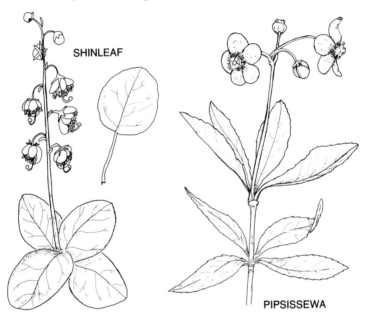

SHINLEAF

PIPSISSEWA

Pipsissewa, Prince's Pine, *Chimaphila umbellata*. This beautiful little evergreen plant has clusters of waxy-petaled hanging flowers on pinkish stems above the narrow, leathery, dark green leaves. The finely toothed leaves, 2.5-6 cm (1-2.5 in) long, are arranged in whorls or clusters on the stems, not basal as in most Wintergreens. The petals are pink to white, each concave and standing outwards, showing off the ten stamens with dilated hairy filaments. Found in moist pine woods and along streams and in the mountains over much of the United States. In the east they grow from Canada into the northern states, south in the mountains to Georgia, west to northern Illinois.

Chapter VIII

FIVE SEPARATE PETALS
NOT ALL ALIKE

Many plants which have five separate petals not all alike are common garden plants, so they are familiar to everybody. They include the large Pea Family and the Violet Family.

PEA FAMILY
Leguminosae or *Fabaceae*

The blossoms of Sweet Peas and beans are so familiar that nearly everyone knows them. Most members of this family have the same characteristic blossoms, with five more or less united sepals forming a cup and five separate petals. The large upper one is called the "standard" or "banner," and covers the others in the bud. The two side petals are called "wings." The lowest petal is called a "keel" but it is really two petals lightly stuck together. Hiding inside the keel are the ten stamens. Often nine stamens, sometimes all ten, have united filaments, making a collar around the ovary and curved style. The superior ovary is one-celled; the pod is two-sided, with many seeds. (Peas and beans are excellent examples of the seed pods.) This pod is called a legume, and is characteristic of the family, whether they are herbs, vines, shrubs, or trees. Common members of food plants are: peas, beans, licorice for humans; alfalfa, clover, and vetch for animals. Locust and Redbud are examples of trees that belong to this family. Although we have many edible legumes, some wild members, like the lupines, are poisonous, especially the seeds.

Red Clover, *Trifolium pratense,* paints whole fields and road-sides with its deep red or purplish (or even almost white) color all over the east. The fragrant, pea-like flowers, with the banner often creased, are tiny but many grow in a dense, large, round head. The leaves are the well-known clover leaves of three leaflets—quite pointed. They are blue-green with wide V-shaped lighter areas. Both stems and leaves are soft and lightly hairy to the touch. The plant may grow as tall as a meter (3 ft), the lower leaves long-stalked.

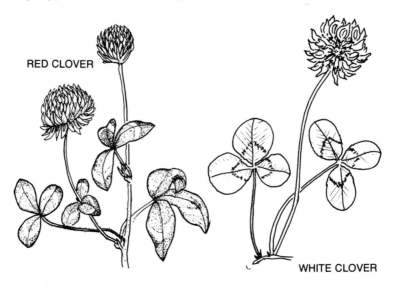

RED CLOVER

WHITE CLOVER

White Clover, *Trifolium repens,* is the common white clover of roadsides and lawns, with similar large round flower heads somewhat creamy in color. It is a low creeping plant with quite round or heart-shaped green leaflets (often you can find four- or five-leafed clovers on plants of this species). The stems and leaves are not fuzzy or hairy. The V-shaped lighter areas on leaflets may or may not be as distinct as in Red Clover.

Hop Clover, *Trifolium aureum,* is an annual clover with tiny
yellow flowers in a head. As the flowers wither, they fade to tan
and turn downwards, resembling tiny groups of dried hops. It is
a slender, branching plant, with small, slender leaflets. It is
quite similar to the Bur Clovers or Medicks, but its pod is
straight, not spirally twisted. It can be found from the east
coast west to Iowa along roadsides.

HOP CLOVER

WOOD VETCH

Wood Vetch, Carolina Vetch, *Vicia caroliniana.* The vetches are
small, trailing plants with pinnately compound leaves, the end
leaflet modified to form a tendril. Usually they have lavender,
pinkish, or whitish flowers. Wood or Carolina Vetch is a common species not only in the Carolinas, but from New York to
Georgia to Oklahoma, growing along roads and shores. It has
six to twelve pairs of leaflets, the small flower (1 cm) is whitish,
sometimes with a bit of blue. There are many different vetches,
low-growing or twining, and all very pretty.

Beach Pea, Vetchling, *Lathyrus maritus*. This genus resembles the vetches in leaf and tendril but has larger blossoms and big stipules. The flowers of Beach Pea are bluish, pink-lavender, or purplish, and are more than 2.5 cm (1 in) across. The plant is a slender, climbing plant which clings to others with its tendrils—the tendrils at the end of each compound leaf. Each leaf has six to twelve oval leaflets. There are large, arrow-shaped stipules at the base of the compound leaves. Can be found on beaches of New England and southward to New Jersey and around the Great Lakes.

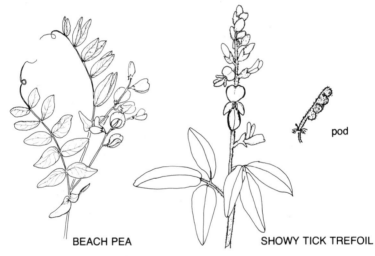

pod

BEACH PEA   SHOWY TICK TREFOIL

Showy Tick-Trefoil, Bush Tick-Trefoil, Sticktights, *Desmodium canescens,* is one of the many Tick-Trefoils in the east. All are much alike, with small, typically pea-shaped flowers in clusters or racemes. This red-purple flower is about 2 cm across in clusters at the top of a hairy, leafy branch. The branching, hairy plant may be a meter (3 ft) or more tall, the compound leaves having three long, oval leaflets. The pod is deeply lobed on its lower side and has tiny hooked hairs. The pods are at least three times as long as the sepals and will easily break apart between the lobes and will stick to clothing and animal fur, thus spreading to new locations. This Sticktight grows in moist spots from Canada to Virginia, west to Ohio and Oklahoma, flowering in the summer.

Groundnut or Wild Bean, *Apios americana,* gets its common name from the little "nuts" which are tuberous enlargements of the roots. These are edible, with a sweet flavor even when raw, and also good cooked. They grow in woods and damp fields from Canada to Florida, west to Minnesota, flowering all summer. The deep pink pea flowers (lighter color on the outside) grow in thick clusters on a stem from the leaf axils. The fruit is a bean-like pod.

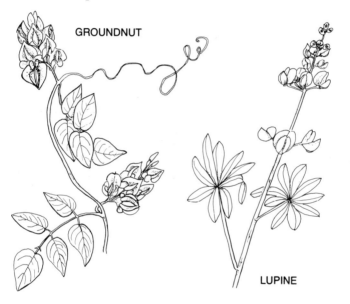

GROUNDNUT

LUPINE

Lupine, *Lupinus perennis,* grows to 60 cm (2 ft) tall in open sandy areas from Maine to Florida, west to Missouri and Minnesota. The pea-like flowers usually are blue, but may be violet or purplish, the veined banner lighter in color. They grow in a spike. The leaves are palmately compound with seven to nine leaflets; they and the stem are lightly hairy. The fruit is a pod, the seeds *poisonous.* There are two eastern Lupines: *Lupinus villosus* with such soft hairy leaves they appear silverish and lilac flowers with dark spots; *Lupinus diffusus* with green, downy leaves, and blue flowers with yellowish spots on the banner. The Bluebonnet, state flower of Texas, is a Lupine, and there are many that grow in the west.

HOARY PEA

Hoary Pea or Goat's Rue, *Tephrosia virginiana,* is a widespread large hairy plant with numerous flowers about 2 cm across (1 in) in a raceme. Each flower has a yellow banner, the wings and keel of red, pinkish, or deep lavender. The wings and keel stick together. The leaves are pinnately compound, each of the fifteen to twenty-five leaflets 2.5 cm or more long. Both they and the stems are covered with white, silky hairs. Grows to 60 cm (24 in) tall in sandy areas from New England to Florida, west to Texas.

VIOLET FAMILY
Violaceae

Violets are one of our best-known wildflowers, and the garden species are much like the wild ones. There are hundreds of species all over the world, with fifty-one different ones in the east! (We've included the thirteen most common.) They may be blue, lavender, white, yellow, purple, or a combination, and there is considerable variation. Most of the seeds are produced late in the season by special flowers close to, or even under, the ground. The late flowers may lack petals and are self-pollinating. Violets have stipules at leaf bases, sometimes quite large. There are five sepals which persist, protecting the capsule. The five petals are irregular, with two upper ones alike, two side ones alike, and one lower petal with a spur or nectar sac at its base. None or some of the petals may be bearded at the throat. The five stamens with short, broad filaments are placed tightly over the plump, ten-celled ovary. The walls of the ripe ovary curl open into three parts with such force that the seeds are popped out a meter or two. Violets usually grow from perennial rootstalks. Violets are state flowers for Illinois, Rhode Island, Wisconsin, and New Jersey. Some species have flowers on leafless (naked) stems, leaves on their own stem; others have leafy flowering stems. We separate them that way.

Leafless Flowering-stemmed Violets

Birdfoot Violet, Wild Pansy, *Viola pedata,* is one of the largest violets, with flowers 2.5 cm (1 in) or more across, the upper petals flaring back. It carpets roadsides, meadows, and woods from New England to Virginia, and west into Arkansas. The flowers stand on their own stem. One variety, Velvets, has the two upper petals a darker color than the others. All the petals are blue-purple or deep lilac, the spurred petal having a white spot near the throat. The orange stamens are easily seen in this species. The dull pale green leaves give the plant its common name, for they are deeply divided into at least three lobes, which are again divided and cleft. It flowers from March to June.

BIRDFOOT VIOLET

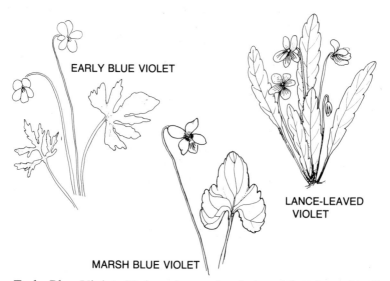

EARLY BLUE VIOLET

LANCE-LEAVED
VIOLET

MARSH BLUE VIOLET

Early Blue Violet, *Viola palmata,* is a hairy violet also with divided leaves, each having five to eleven lobes, the side and middle lobes larger. The flowers are about 2.5 cm across and light blue or violet-blue in color, the lowest petal bearded. This violet grows in dry wooded hills all over the east.

Marsh Blue Violet, *Viola cucullata,* is pale blue-lavender with a dark purple center and dark veins. The flowers are on longer stalks than the leaves. The lowest petal is veined but not bearded and is shorter than the two side petals which have dense beards. The leaves are heart-shaped, the margins of the young leaves rolled inward. They grow to be 5-10 cm (2-4 in) wide. This violet grows in marshes, near streams, and in wet meadows all through New England and south to Georgia, flowering till June.

Lance-leaved Violet, *Viola lanceolata,* is a small white violet with purple stripes or veins on the lower three petals and no beard. The leaves are lance-shaped 5-15 cm (2-6 in) long and only about 2 cm wide. They stand erect, sometimes nearly hiding the flowers. It is found throughout the east and west to Minnesota from March to July in swamps and wet meadows.

Coast Violet, *V. brittoniana,* has large (2.5-3 cm, 1+ in) flowers of a deep purple with a white throat. The three lower petals have dense beards, the lowest petal with darker purple veins. The leaves are three-parted with the segments again cleft, the middle division always bigger. These grow in damp soils along the coast from Maine to Virginia, into the mountains of the south from May to July.

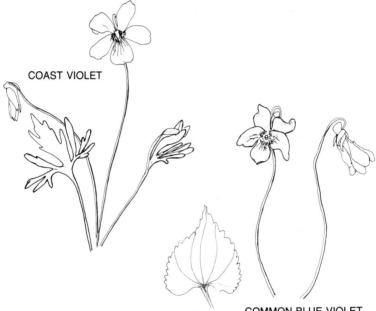

COAST VIOLET

COMMON BLUE VIOLET

Common Blue Violet, *Viola papilionacea,* is also called Meadow Violet because it grows so thickly in some areas it is difficult not to walk on it. It can usually be found around homes and pastures. It has large, heart-shaped leaves with scalloped margins, the deep blue flowers standing on their own stalks usually above the leaves. The spurred petal is fairly narrow, the side petals wear white beards at the throat. It is found all through the east. The Confederate Violet, *Viola papilionacea* (var. *princeana*) is a variety of the Common Blue Violet. It is a large grayish-white flower, the lower petals marked near the center with lavender areas and dark veins.

Leafy Flowering-stemmed Violets

Pale or Striped Violet, *Viola striata,* has deep green, heart-shaped leaves with large toothed stipules at base of leaves. The white or creamy flowers grow on the same stalk as the leaves. The lateral petals are bearded, the broad lowest petal striped with purple. This plant grows 15-30 cm (6-12 in) tall in woods and fields from New York to Georgia, west to Minnesota and Missouri, flowering from April to June.

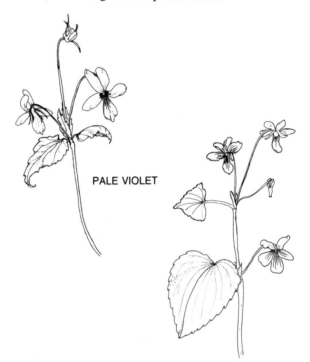

PALE VIOLET

YELLOW VIOLET

Yellow Violet, *Viola pensylvanica,* is a bright yellow violet with purple stripes on the lower three petals. The leaves are heart-shaped and stand erect, sometimes hiding the flowers which are on the same stem. It is found throughout the east from March to July in swamps and wet meadows.

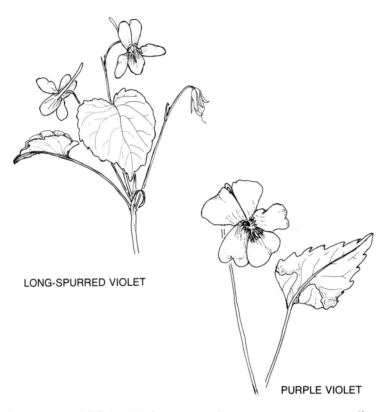

LONG-SPURRED VIOLET

PURPLE VIOLET

Long-spurred Violet, *Viola rostrata,* has a one-cm spur extending
behind the flower—an elongation of the lowest petal. The
flower is pale lavender (sometimes white) with a dark center,
not bearded. There are dark lines on all the petals. The leaves
are heart-shaped, smooth, and slightly serrate on the edges. It
is a shady hillside and moist wood violet, found all over the east
blooming in spring.

Purple Violet, *Viola adunca,* is a plain purple violet with darker
purple lines on the lowest petal. The leaves are heart-shaped
and basal, on stems shorter than those of the flowers. They are
long and weak so they tend to lie on the ground. This violet
grows from Canada and New England westward to Oregon and
California.

Canada Violet, *Viola canadensis,* has small white flowers with
yellow centers, purplish on the backside, the lower three petals
purple-veined, the side ones also bearded. The heart-shaped
leaves are 2-3 cm long, growing on the same strong, hairy,
purplish stems as the flowers. It may grow to 30 cm (1 ft).
These violets are very plentiful in eastern Canada and grow
southward to South Carolina in the mountains.

CANADA VIOLET

FIELD PANSY

Field Pansy, Johnny-Jump-Up, *Viola rafinesquii,* is a spring annual growing in fields and along roads from New York to Georgia, west to Texas and Colorado. The flowers are small,
creamy, or bluish-white, often marked with yellow. The
spoon-shaped leaves are small, on slender petioles with large,
conspicuous, deeply cut stipules. Flowers and leaves are on the
same stalk.

Chapter IX

FIVE UNITED PETALS ALL ALIKE

Many flowers have five united petals, all alike. Often the petals are united only at the base, but many have petals that are bell- or funnel-shaped. Some have distinct petal lobes, others are so united they appear as a single circular petal, but all have lines or markings which show there are five united petals.

MORNING GLORY FAMILY
Convolvulaceae

This family was given its Latin name because it means "to twist," and most members of this family are vines or creeping plants and the petals are twisted in the bud. The flowers are well-known, with the corolla often very showy, opening in the morning hours. The five sepals are separate and persist to protect the capsule, the five united petals are funnel-shaped, and the pistil is two-celled. The parasitic plant, Dodder, belongs to this family, as can be seen from its flower structure. It produces no green parts and depends on the plant it twines around and into for its food. It looks like yellow-orange string winding and trailing over, under, and through other plants. Sweet Potato also belongs to this family.

Hedge Bindweed, *Convolvulus sepium*, is common all over the east and west to New Mexico. Its sprawling vines cover fences, walk, and banks. It has simple, long-stalked, arrowhead-shaped leaves (or with an angular base) that are alternate. The funnel-shaped flowers are 5-7.5 cm (2-3 in) across, white or rosy-pink. There are two bracts below (and almost enclosing) the calyx. Upright or Low Bindweed, *Convolvulus spithameus*, has a flower which looks much the same, but the plant is short and may grow upright or sprawl over the ground a bit, not twine everywhere. The leaves are oblong, often heart-shaped at base, with a short stalk.

Wild Potato-vine, *Ipomoea pandurata*, actually was used by Indians as a substitute for potatoes, but its more bitter flavor kept it from being used much by pioneers. This plant develops huge roots, as long as five meters (15 ft) and may weigh as much as six or seven kilos (15 lbs). The white flowers are large and showy, about 7.5 cm (3 in) across with a pink or red stripe down each petal lobe; the center may be purple. There are no bracts below the sepals. The large leaves are often heart-shaped. This vine grows from New England to Florida, west to Texas.

Common or Tall Morning Glory, *Ipomoea purpurea*, is an escaped garden vine in the United States, but a native to tropical America. The showy flowers may be pink, red, purple, blue, or white, and are commonly variegated, often with three or more flowers in an umbel. The leaves are heart-shaped. It can be found all over the east.

HEDGE BINDWEED

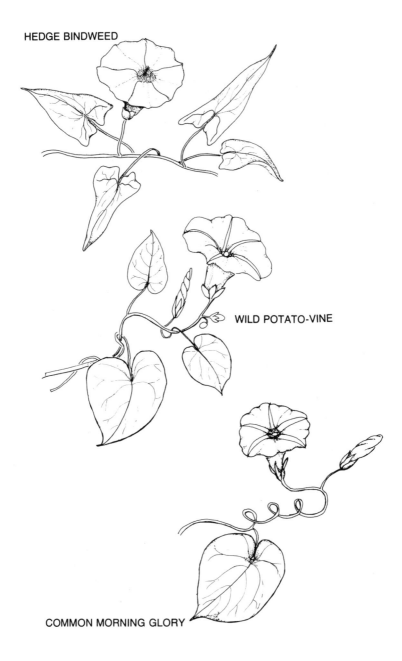

WILD POTATO-VINE

COMMON MORNING GLORY

GENTIAN FAMILY
Gentianaceae

Gentians usually are small herbs with an odorless but bitter juice. The opposite leaves are smooth-margined and sessile. The sepals are fused except at the tip, and are five-toothed (sometimes four). The petals are united into a corolla tube, with the lobes free, and are of the same number as the calyx lobes. The corolla lobes overlap or twist in the bud. The five stamens alternate with the petal lobes and are attached to the throat of the corolla. The superior ovary has two stigmas, the seeds in a capsule, the corolla remaining and drying. The flowers may be deep blue, yellow, rose-pink, or green-white.

Fringed Gentian, a very common Gentian of the east, has four petals, not five, so is included in Chapter VI.

Closed Gentian or Bottle Gentian, *Gentiana andrewsii,* is peculiar in that its petals never open, but remain closed as if in bud. There is a whitish membrane which connects (and is actually longer than) the five petals. This membrane is tightly plaited, thus closing the petals. The flowers grow in dense clusters at the stem top and in the axils of the upper, opposite leaves. The plants are 60-120 cm (2-4 ft) tall, with thick stems and long leaves with pointed tips. Each flower is surrounded by two

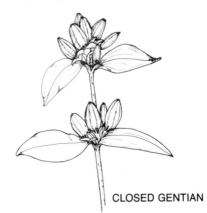

CLOSED GENTIAN

leafy green bracts. The flowers usually are deep blue, whitish towards the base, but may be purple, pinkish, or white. They grow from Canada into New England to Georgia, west to Arkansas, flowering from August to October.

Pine-barren Gentian, *Gentiana autumnalis* (*porphyrio*), grows along the damp coastal areas from New Jersey to South Carolina. It may be 30-60 cm (1-2 ft) tall. There are solitary (sometimes two or three) flowers at the tips of the stems. Five fringed subordinate parts alternate with the five pointed long petal lobes, which may seem to make this Gentian have ten petals. The flowers are blue with paler stripes and specks, the tube portion brownish, or the flower may be greenish-white or brownish. The opposite leaves are very narrow and pointed.

PINE-BARREN GENTIAN   MARSH ROSE-GENTIAN

Marsh Rose-Gentian, Marsh-pink, *Sabatia stellaris*. All species of *Sabatia* are found in the southeast. They usually have five petals (but some have several). This star-like flower has its five pink petals only lightly joined at the base so they need careful examination or they will be mistaken for separate petals. The flowers, about 2.5 cm (1 in) across, are terminal at branch tips. They have a yellow "eye," bordered with red. The leaves are oblong, fairly slender, becoming quite small near the top of the stem. They grow in salt marshes along the coast from Massachusetts to Florida, blooming over a long period of time.

PRIMROSE FAMILY
Primulaceae

All Primroses are plants with five petals united at least at the base, and with simple, undivided leaves. The stamens are opposite the petals (standing in front of each lobe), not alternate as with most flowers. There is a single style and stigma. The flowers are perfect, regular, symmetrical, on the plan of five, with a superior ovary. The fruit is a capsule. The lovely Primroses and Cyclamens which grow in gardens are favorites in this family.

Scarlet Pimpernel, *Anagallis arvensis*, really is more of a deep coral color than scarlet. It opens only in sunny weather. It is a small flower, not quite 1 cm across, growing on weak, angular stems which may be a foot long (30 cm). The small opposite leaves are entire and sessile. The five rounded petals are joined just at the base, and often have a darker color band in the center. The calyx is deeply divided into five narrow lobes. The fruit is a round capsule which opens with a lid. Though a lovely flower, it also grows in lawns and gardens everywhere, so some consider it a pest. Scarlet Pimpernel grows all over America, and is an introduced weed from Europe. A blue variety may be found.

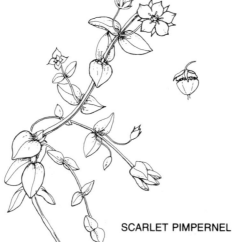

SCARLET PIMPERNEL

Bird's-eye Primrose, *Primula mistassinica*. This dainty flower looks very much like the garden species and grows from Canada to New York and westward across the northern states. It is a small plant with a basal rosette of somewhat blunt leaves. The single flowering stalk produces an umbel of small pink or lilac flowers at the top. The five notched petals, with a yellow center, spread out from their tube, each flower 2-2.5 cm (.75-1 in) across.

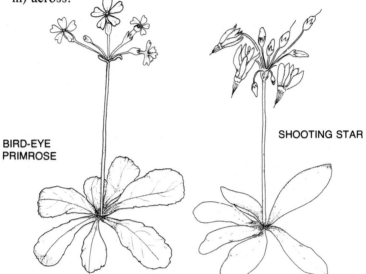

BIRD-EYE PRIMROSE

SHOOTING STAR

Shooting Star, Mosquito Bills, *Dodecatheon meadia*. The blossoms of Shooting Star seem turned inside out, for the corolla and calyx are deeply cut and turn back away from the stamens and pistil. Several magenta, lavender-pink, or sometimes white flowers grow in an umbel on the top of a slender stem. Usually there are bands of white, yellow, or purple at the base of the petals. The stamens with thick filaments closely surround the single pistil. These parts often look like a beak or bill, so Mosquito Bills is also a common name. The flowers point downwards toward the thick basal rosette of leaves, which are reddish at their base. As the petals fade and drop, the capsule turns up, the calyx still protecting it. These plants grow 30-45 cm (12-18 in) tall in meadows and open woods from Virginia to Georgia, west to Texas. Many similar species grow in the west.

GILIA or PHLOX FAMILY
Polemoniaceae

Most members of this family are herbs, although some develop woody bases. Most of them have small flowers. Leaves vary in size and shape, often are opposite. The five-part calyx is persistent, and the five-lobed or five-pointed corolla is tubular at the base and twisted in the bud. Stamens are attached to the corolla tube, alternate with the lobes. There are three stigmas, and the superior ovary develops into a three-celled capsule with many seeds. This is an American family, with most of its species in the west. There are also many garden species.

Moss Pink, *Phlox subulata*, is not a true Pink, for the petals are united. It has vivid pink (or lavender) blossoms about 1 cm (.5 in) wide, growing in masses on spreading plants. The notched petal lobes are wedge-shaped. The small leaves are linear or needle-like, about 2 cm long (1 in). Moss Pinks can be found in sandy woods from New York to North Carolina and west to Michigan, south to Florida and Kentucky, from March to June.

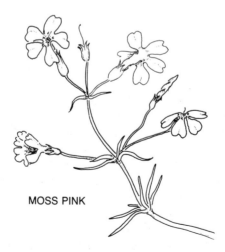

MOSS PINK

Wild Blue Phlox, *Phlox divaricata*, is a flower with hairy, sticky stems and leaves. Each flower is 2-3 cm (1+ in) across, the petal lobes wedge-shaped and may be notched. The stems spread, then turn upwards, the flowers in terminal clusters of bluish-pink, making a mass of color. The stamens are completely hidden. Wild Blue Phlox grows in rocky damp woods from Canada through New England to Alabama, west to Minnesota and Nebraska.

WILD BLUE PHLOX   DOWNEY PHLOX

Downy Phlox, *Phlox pilosa*, looks much like Wild Blue Phlox, except its blossoms are a lovely pink to rose, to violet in color, the stamens hidden. Its stems have a soft, downy covering, the leaves tapering to a very sharp point. It grows 30 cm (12 in) or more tall in sandy areas from New England to Florida, west to Texas.

Wild Sweet William, *Phlox maculata*, has a raceme of large pink or reddish-purple flowers with long corolla tubes at the top of a slender, purple-spotted stem. The opposite leaves are pointed. The plants are about 30-60 cm (1-2 ft) or more tall in woods and damp meadows, and along streams, from Pennsylvania to Minnesota, south to Florida and Arkansas from May to September.

WILD SWEET WILLIAM   GREEK VALERIAN

Greek Valerian or Jacob's Ladder, *Polemonium reptans*, has leaves that are different from the phlox. These are pinnately compound with five to fifteen leaflets each about 2-3 cm (1 in) long. The nodding, bell-like flowers are bluish-purple or blue, 2-3 cm across, growing in racemes. The five stamens do not project out of the corolla tube. This grows in damp areas from Vermont west to Minnesota, south to Alabama and Missouri, flowering from May to July. American Jacob's Ladder, *Polemonium van-bruntiae*, is very similar, but taller, with stronger stems and the stamens projecting from the corolla tube. It is not as common and is found mainly in the mountains.

PHACELIA or WATERLEAF FAMILY
Hydrophyllaceae

Different members of the Phacelia Family may bloom singly on a stem, in heads, or in coiled spikes. The individual blossoms, however, are very similar. The five petals are united at the base, thus the corolla appears cup-like or saucer-like. The five long stamens are attached near the base of the corolla. The superior ovary is two-celled; in some there is just one style that is divided at the tip while in others there are two distinct styles, never three as in the Phlox Family. The leaves are of various shapes, opposite or alternate. The plants usually are quite hairy, and are a favorite of bees. This family is particularly abundant in the west.

White Fringed Phacelia, *Phacelia fimbriata*, grows in great masses, sometimes covering acres with their unusual and lovely creamy blossoms. From a distance they look like snow beds. The flowers are 2-3 cm (1 in) across with very fringed petals, joined only at the base. The leaves are alternate, the lower ones deeply three- to five-lobed, the leaves, stems and calyx hairy. The plants grow only 20-30 cm (8-12 in) tall and are found in woods and mountains, from Virginia to Alabama, and are especially abundant in the Appalachian Mountains.

WHITE FRINGED PHACELIA

Broad-leaved Waterleaf, *Hydrophyllum canadense*, has tiny white to pale flowers with the five stamens protruding so they are the most attractive part; however, the flowers are lower than the leaves on the plant. The palmately five- to seven-lobed leaves are somewhat hairy or may be smooth, heart-shaped at the base. This flower grows in woods of New England, south to Missouri and Alabama. The Large-leaved Waterleaf, *Hydrophyllum macrophyllum*, is very similar, but the toothed, maple-like leaves are nine to thirteen lobed, the flowers whitish-pink and the plants rough-hairy.

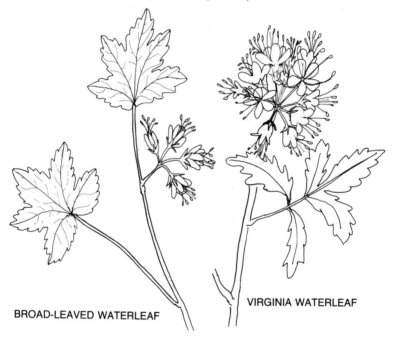

BROAD-LEAVED WATERLEAF

VIRGINIA WATERLEAF

Virginia Waterleaf, *Hydrophyllum virginianum*. The conspicuous, long, projecting stamens are the noticed feature of these small purple or white flowers. They are in terminal heads on slender plants 30-60 cm (1-2 ft) tall. Both the calyx and the stems are hairy, but the hairs lie flat on the stems. The leaves are pinnately divided, usually into five (or seven) toothed, sharply pointed lobes. Virginia Waterleaf grows in wet woods from New England to Virginia, west to Arkansas and Kansas.

BORAGE FAMILY
Boraginaceae

Members of the Borage Family have rather small flowers growing along one-sided, coiled spikes, resembling the neck of a fiddle, and are similar to some members of the Phacelia Family. The stems unroll as the buds open. The family resembles the Phacelias also with hairy stems and leaves, but the ovary develops into nutlets which break apart when ripe—the primary characteristic of the Borages. These nutlets are distinctly separate even in the flower. The leaves are simple and alternate. Forget-me-not and the fragrant Heliotrope are garden species, and most of the wild members resemble them. Forget-me-not is the state flower of Alaska.

Bluebells or Virginia Cowslip, *Mertensia virginica*, is a lovely blue flower growing in a raceme of drooping, bell-like blossoms. The plants may be many centimeters tall (30-90 cm, 1-3 ft) with fairly stout stems, the leaves alternate. The raceme is coiled in bud, but uncoils as the flowers open. The buds are pink, but the opened flowers are blue (sometimes the withered flowers also pinkish). Grows in woods and wet meadows from New York to Alabama, west to Kansas.

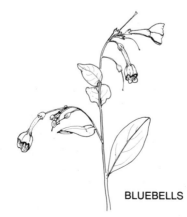

BLUEBELLS

Hound's Tongue or Sheep-lice, *Cynoglossum officinale*, earned its common names because of the leaf shape and the prickly nutlets which tangle in sheep wool. It is magenta-colored and grows all over America from Quebec to the Pacific, south to Arkansas. The flowers seem to stay cup-shaped, and do not open flat. The nutlets open out flat, but stay attached to the base of the style till dry, their surfaces covered with barbed hairs. The flowering coil keeps growing as seeds mature, so the persistent nutlets are scattered on a long spray.

Forget-me-not, *Myosotis scorpioides,* is an escaped garden flower which has established itself as a common wildflower all over damp areas of the east and north into Canada, especially along streams. The little blue flowers, with five dainty united petals, are on a coiled, branched raceme. The center of the flower is yellow with a circle of scales. The angular stem and alternate sessile leaves are somewhat hairy. *Myosotis laxa* is a native species, very similar, but smaller and often growing right in the water.

Yellow Puccoon, *Lithospermum incisum*, has little yellow funnel-shaped flowers with ruffly edges growing in a one-sided raceme, with hairy calyxes. The stems and very narrow leaves are also densely hairy. This perennial grows mostly in the mid-west on the prairies, but can be found in sandy open woods from Canada to British Columbia, south to Indiana, Missouri and Texas. *Lithospermum canescens* is a much yellower puccoon, with smooth-edged petals, shorter corolla tube, and is densely white-hairy.

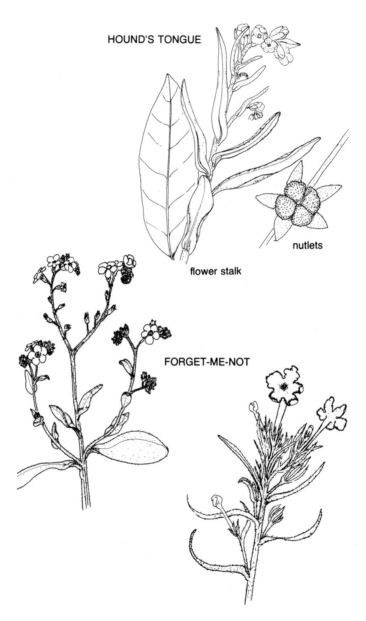

HOUND'S TONGUE

nutlets

flower stalk

FORGET-ME-NOT

YELLOW PUCCOON

NIGHTSHADE FAMILY
Solanaceae

Nightshades grow all over the world, but are especially abundant in the tropics. Some of our best-known foods belong to this family, including potatoes, tomatoes, eggplant, bell peppers, chilies and cayenne peppers. However, some wild species of this family have at least somewhat poisonous berries, especially when unripe. Petunias are familiar garden flower members; also included is tobacco. All have a five-lobed corolla, folded in the bud; some are funnel-shaped but most are saucer-like. The five almost sessile stamens are inserted on the corolla, alternately with its lobes, and usually stand together in a tight cluster. The two-celled superior ovary has one style and a one- or two-lobed stigma. The fruit is a berry or capsule.

Common Nightshade, *Solanum nigrum*, has white or even yellowish flowers. The plants have many branches, with the flowers in loose umbels blooming over a long season, so there may be buds, flowers, and berries all at the same time. The Common Nightshade is found in fields and open places over most of the United States and southern Canada and is also called the Black Nightshade. It was introduced from Europe and the small whitish star-like flower one cm across develops into a black berry.

COMMON NIGHTSHADE

flower

Horse-nettle, *Solanum carolinense*, is a common weed with flowers similar to the Common Nightshade, but the lobes are wider,
the white or pale lavender blossoms a little larger. The leaves
are rough, lobed, or with occasional teeth along the margins.
The stems and the midveins on the underside of leaves have
stout yellow prickles. The berries are yellow to orangish.
Grows 30-120 cm (1-4 ft) tall in fields and wild from Canada
south through New York to Florida and west into Iowa to
Texas.

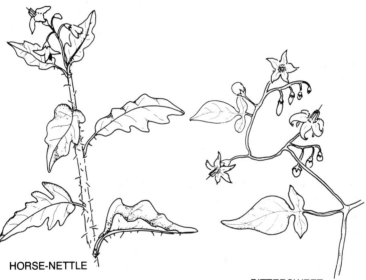

HORSE-NETTLE

BITTERSWEET

Bittersweet, *Solanum dulcamara*, has berries of such a characteristic orange-red color (when ripe) that bittersweet is considered the name of a color. The berries are more familiar to most
people than its little purple (or lighter) star-like flowers, with
the petals swept back from the beak-like stamens. Beautiful
though the berries are, they are considered *poisonous*. The
leaves have two ear-like lobes below the main blade. This is
another escaped European plant which grows as a trailing,
softly-hairy vine in moist areas all over the east.

JIMSON WEED

Jimson Weed, Jamestown Weed, Thorn Apple, *Datura stramonium*, is a very *poisonous* weed which grows in waste areas all over the United States. It is a stout plant growing to one and half meters (3-4.5 ft) tall. The trumpet-shaped flowers with sharply-pointed lobes are white or light violet, and may be 5-10 cm (2-4 in) across. The large leaves have wavy edges with a few teeth. The fruit is a prickly capsule with large flat seeds.

MILKWEED FAMILY
Asclepidaceae

Milkweeds are summer-blooming plants with milky juice, opposite, whorled, or alternate leaves, with their many intricate, unique flowers in umbels. The calyx is small, the five sepal lobes turned backwards but are covered by the five petal lobes, which are also reflexed when the flower is open. In the middle stands a crown-like structure (called a corona). This is made up of five little cups which support five tiny horns that curve into the center where the stamens and shield-like stigma are united into a structure. The tips of the five stamens are supported by two styles. The pollen of each stamen is in two waxy masses. Adjoining pollen masses are attached to deeply divided glands. If an insect's leg slips into one of the clefts, the two pollen sacs, hanging like saddle bags by a connecting thread, are lifted out, and will be carried to the next flower. Seeds are produced in long, pointed pods. The seeds are flat and packed in overlapping rows, each with long, silky, white hairs.

Butterfly Weed, *Asclepias tuberosa*, is a common, strikingly beautiful plant in dry fields, blooming from July to September everywhere, but especially abundant in the southern areas. The stems are very leafy, branching near the tip and producing many umbels of bright orange or yellow intricate-appearing flowers. The sessile, opposite leaves are light olive-green, 5-15 cm long and 1-2.5 cm wide (2-6 in, .3-1 in). The 30-60 cm (1-2 ft) stem is rough and hairy. The erect, slender, pointed pod, on an S-shaped stem, is filled with many flat seeds, each with white, silky hairs. Given its common name because the monarch butterfly lays its eggs on this plant and the striped caterpillar feeds on its leaves.

BUTTERFLY WEED   COMMON MILKWEED

Common Milkweed, *Asclepias syriaca*, is found everywhere, especially in the northern areas, blooming from July through September. The tall, stout, soft-hairy stem may be 60-150 cm tall (2-5 ft). The soft, thick, broadly oval leaves, with a long point, are opposite and may be 10-20 cm long or longer (4-8+ in). There are numerous umbels from the upper leaf axils—each with many rose-lavender or purplish-brown intricate flowers. The flowers are somewhat sweet. The young shoots can be cooked as "greens." The thin, overlapping seeds, each with its tuft of long silky down, are in a rough, warty pod. *Asclepias purpurescens* is similar, but the flowers are maroon-red or crimson, with broad, pointed-in horns in the flower's corona. Common from Maine to Georgia, and west to Minnesota.

BLUEBELL FAMILY
Campanulaceae

The Bluebell or *Campanulaceae* Family has now been expanded to include the Lobelia Family, so botanists now give it two subfamilies, those to which the Bluebells belong (the *Campanuloideae*), and that which includes the Lobelias (*Lobelioideae*).

The *Campanulaceae* is a widely distributed family, mostly herbs, with five-parted calyx, five-parted corolla, five stamens and an inferior ovary, the calyx tube fused to the ovary and only the tips free. The fruit is usually a capsule. The leaves are alternate and simple. The Bluebell subfamily generally has hanging, bell-like flowers, usually blue (but may be purple, white, or pink). The corolla lobes are alike and the five stamens are attached to the corolla where the calyx tips are free. The ovary is two- to five-celled, with one style but two to five stigmas. There are many garden flowers that are in this family, such as Canterbury Bells, Harebells, etc.

The members of the Lobelia subfamily are very different in one respect—they have a two-lipped corolla, the petals not all the same shape. Therefore, we will include it in the next chapter, where you will find a write-up of its distinctive characteristics. The juice of both subfamilies is milky and more or less *poisonous*.

Harebell or Bluebell, *Campanula rotundifolia*, has rounded, heart-shaped small basal leaves which wither early. The stem leaves are long and slender. The nodding flowers have spreading lobes—they really look much like dainty little bells on wiry, hair-like stems. This little flower is found in Europe as well as America, and is the Bluebell of Scotland. It grows in dry sandy meadows, on cliffs, and beaches among the grasses all over the northern part of America.

Tall Bellflowers, *Campanula americana,* grows one to two meters tall (3-6 ft), on stout, somewhat hairy stems. The showy,
very light blue flowers with a pale eye ring are 3 cm or more (1+
in) across, growing in the axils of the upper leaves. The flowers
are flat, except for the short tubular basal portion of the corolla,
not the typical "bell-shape." The style is long and curving, first
down, then up, extending past the outer edge of the flower; it is
tipped by the 3-parted stigma. The thin, somewhat hairy serrate
leaves are oval, but taper to a point. The lower ones are narrowed at the base like a stem. They grow in moist woods from
New York to North Dakota, and south to Florida, Georgia,
Arkansas, flowering from June to August or later.

HAREBELLS

TALL BELLFLOWER

FIGWORT FAMILY
Scrophulariaceae

Most members of the Figwort Family have five united pet-als not all alike, and so are included in the next chapter.

However, Mullein, *Verbascum thapsus*, has five corolla lobes which are so much alike that they fit better in this chapter. The two upper lobes are only slightly smaller than the three lower ones. The plant is tall, stiff, unbranched, and semi-woody. The leaves are velvety with soft, thick, white hairs. They are mostly basal and large, forming a beautiful rosette on the ground. In the spring, a tall flower stalk grows with flowers intermixed with progressively smaller leaves tightly attached by half their midvein length along the flowering stalk. The flower head is a closely crowded 12-30 cm (6-12 in) spike, with open, bright yellow little flowers irregularly scattered among the leaves, buds, and maturing capsules. Mullein is found all over the United States along roadsides and on dry slopes up to 8,000 feet elevation.

MULLEIN

Chapter X

FIVE UNITED PETALS NOT ALL ALIKE

Many of our irregular or "queer-shaped" flowers have five petal lobes, but the lobes are not all the same shape, so they fit in this chapter. Most of them have a tubular corolla that is "two-lipped," each lip having two or three lobes. Many of them are very beautiful. The well-known Snapdragons, the Mints, and the Lobelias fit here.

BLUEBELL FAMILY
Campanulaceae

(including *Lobeliaceae*)

The Bluebell Family now includes the Lobelias as a sub-family (*Lobelioideae*). The Lobelias are characterized by having the corolla five-lobed, but the lobes are arranged into two lips, the upper with two lobes, the lower with three. Sometimes the flower turns upside down so it looks as though it is reversed. The filaments of the stamens are fused around the style; often the anthers are also fused. Now comes *the* different feature—the upper lip is split deeply (far more than the lower). The basal half of each lobe bends forward, then the tips stand up or outwards. Along that split, the united stamens and style push, projecting through the gap. The five-parted calyx has narrow lobes, the plants are generally small, and the flowers colorful.

Cardinal Flower, *Lobelia cardinalis,* makes a mass of brilliant red flowers growing on a one to two meter (3-6 ft) plant. The irregular, two-lipped flowers, about 5 cm (2 in) across and shaped somewhat like Orchids, are fabulous to find. The corolla lobes are so narrow and long and the stamens and style that project

CARDINAL FLOWER

between the split upper lip are so red, that the flower appears to have six segments, not five. The stem is unbranched and stout, the leaves alternate. This plant is common throughout the eastern and central states along streams and in moist meadows, from Canada to the Gulf.

MINT FAMILY
Labitae

There are many different mints in the east—many, small-flowered, quite inconspicuous ones, but a few with lovely colorful flowers. A magnifier is often useful. The most dependable clues to members of this family are the square stems, the opposite leaves, and an aromatic odor when the leaves are crushed. The united corolla is two-lipped, usually with two lobes in the upper lip and three in the lower, with the flowers growing in whorls or tight spikes. The calyx is five-toothed and also may be two-lipped. There usually are four stamens, standing in pairs on the corolla tube; sometimes two are sterile, without anthers. The ovary is superior with four lobes, separating into four *smooth* little nutlets, the style ending in a forked stigma. Many members of this family are herbs useful for cooking, like sage and thyme. The unpleasant Stinging Nettles are also members.

Bluecurls, *Trichostema dichotomum.* The four long, blue or purple, arching stamens, extending past the two-lipped corolla, are the recognizable feature of this little, much-branched plant. The flowers are blue (occasionally pinkish or white), growing singly at the tips of the paired branchlets. The upper lip is four-lobed, with the long stamens extending out between the two middle lobes. The lower lip is longer (almost tongue-like), and hangs down. The calyx has four lobes above and one below also. The plant grows 10-70 cm tall (4-30 in). The stems and leaves are somewhat sticky. The opposite leaves are narrow and sessile. Bluecurls can be found in dry fields and woods from Maine to Michigan, south to Florida and west to Texas, flowering July to October. The Bluecurls of the west is a tall plant.

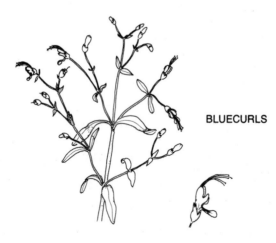

BLUECURLS

Beebalm, Bergamot, Oswego Tea, *Monarda didyma,* is an attractive tall plant with bright scarlet heads at the stem top. The
tight clusters are surrounded by broad bracts, often reddish,
the inner ones quite bristly. Each blossom is about 5 cm (2 in)
long, two-lipped with the upper lip standing upright, and the
lower one wide-spreading. The lower middle lobe is longer than
the other two. Two of the stamens have anthers and project
beyond the upper corolla tube, the other two are undeveloped
and not noticeable. The flowers grow in large dense clusters.
The opposite leaves are hairy, pointed, sharply toothed and
have a definite mint-like fragrance; frequently they are bronzish
in color. It grows from Canada to Georgia, and west to Michigan, generally along streams or in damp areas. *Monarda fis-
tulosa* is very similar but the flowers (and bracts) are pinkish or
lilac-color.

Downy Wood-mint, *Blephilia ciliata,* has small blue-purple, tubular flowers crowded together in successive whorls around the
square stem, each whorl cupped by a row of bracts. The flower
is two-lipped, with the two upper lobes erect, the lower lip with
three spreading lobes, and the throat of the tube swollen. The
stamens project somewhat beyond the tube. The stems and the
undersides of the opposite, almost sessile leaves are extremely
white-downy underneath. The leaves are almost toothless, except the lower ones. Wood-mint grows 30-60 cm (1-2 ft) tall,
and is common in dry woods all over the east from Canada to
the Carolinas, west to Minnesota, Kansas, and Texas, flowering from June to August.

Lyre-leaved Sage, *Salvia lyrata,* has spaced whorls of light purple
tubular flowers which are more showy than most mints—about
two cm or more long (1 in). The upper lip is only slightly divided into two, but the lower lip has three spreading lobes, with
a large middle lobe. The calyx is also two-lipped. The basal
leaves are divided ("like a lyre"), giving the plant its common
name. The square stems are very hairy. This mint grows from
New England to Florida, west to Arkansas and Oklahoma,
flowering from April to June or July.

BEEBALM

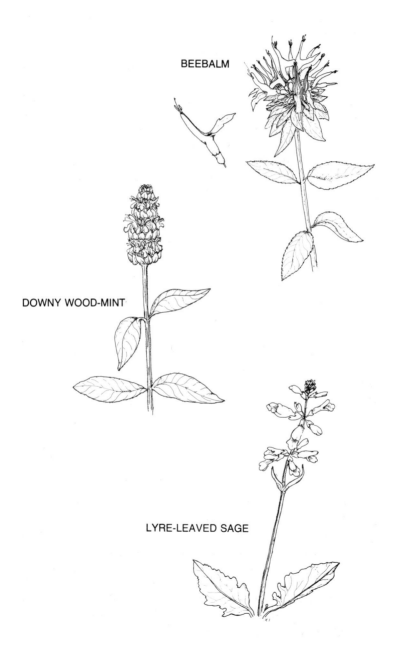

DOWNY WOOD-MINT

LYRE-LEAVED SAGE

Horse-balm, Richweed, Stoneroot, *Collinsonia canadensis,* has numerous delicate, pale yellow flowers, with a bell-shaped, two-lipped calyx. The irregular corolla has four small equal lobes, the fifth (lowest one) is larger and fringed. The two stamens and style are very long. The flowers grow in branching, loose, spreading clusters at the top of the stems, the stout plant may be more than a meter tall (3 ft). The leaves are large and toothed, growing opposite each other up the almost smooth, square stem. This perennial grows in moist woods from New England to Florida to Arkansas, flowering from July to September. The flowers and leaves have a lemon fragrance.

HORSE-BALM

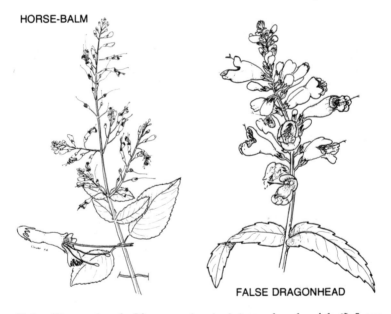

FALSE DRAGONHEAD

False Dragonhead, *Physostegia virginiana,* has largish (2.5 cm, 1 in), showy, pink or pinkish-lavender flowers with a spotted lower lip, resembling Penstemons, growing in a crowded terminal spike 10-20 cm (4-8 in) long. However, the square stems and only four stamens are clues that help identify it as a member of the Mint Family. The tubular corolla is about 2-3 cm (1 in) long, with two upper lobes and three spreading lower ones. They grow in fields and along roads from Canada to Florida, flowering all summer.

Blue Giant Hyssop, *Agastache foeniculum*. The blue flowers are tubular and grow in whorls around the square stem in axils of bracts at intervals up the stem (an "interrupted" spike of flowers). The upper whorls, however, generally are closer together and the spike is not "interrupted." Each flower is two-lipped and has two pairs of protruding stamens. The upper pair points down, the lower pair points upwards (so they cross), with the pistil extending straight out between the pairs. The flowers are about 1 cm long (counting the long stamens). The toothed leaves are woolly on the underside and have a strong odor of anise. This species is found mainly in the prairies. The Yellow Giant Hyssop (*Agastache nepetoides*) is found from Quebec south and has a dense spike of yellowish flowers. The Purple Giant Hyssop (*Agastache scrophulariafolia*) is found from Vermont south, the purplish flowers in crowded spikes with purplish bracts. All species have the same general characteristics, especially the protruding, crossed stamens.

BLUE GIANT HYSSOP   GILL-OVER-THE-GROUND

Gill-over-the-Ground, Ground Ivy, *Glecoma hederacea,* covers banks and areas around old buildings and moist shady spots over much of northern United States. It is a weed from Europe but is a lovely little trailing mint with purple or bluish flowers. Sometimes it becomes a pest in lawns and gardens. The blossoms are trumpet-shaped, and grow in the axils of the scalloped, round, or kidney-shaped opposite leaves on upright short branches. Each flower is about 2 cm (.75 in) long with a narrow upper lip; the lower lip has three spreading lobes spotted with dark purple. The calyx is very fine-hairy. Gill-over-the-Ground may bloom from March through May.

Self-heal, *Prunella vulgaris,* is a very common wildflower all over America and southern Canada, making large patches of purple (sometimes whitish) in fields and along roads. The flowers are tubular and have a two-parted upper lip which is hoodlike over the two pairs of upright stamens and the pistil. The three lobes of the lower lip are bent sharply down and are fringed. The calyx is somewhat purplish and is deeply two-lipped, somewhat fringed. The flowers are crowded among reddish, square-ended, slightly fringed bracts, forming a squarish or oblong head. The leaves are variable but generally are oval and almost smooth margined. The hairy square stems are slender, the plant spreading, low-growing, or even creeping. It flowers from May to October.

SELF-HEAL

MAD-DOG SKULLCAP

Mad-dog Skullcap, Blue Skullcap, *Scutellaria lateriflora.* There are many species of this genus in the east. All have a peculiar hump on the upper surface of the calyx. The flower is tiny, the upper lip hood-like, the two side lobes joined high on the upper lip, and the lower lip is flat. They are not aromatic plants as are most mints, but are bitter. This species is characterized by its violet (may be pink or white) flowers arranged in small racemes in leaf axils on just one side of the stem, as species name suggests, often with tiny leaves. The small green cup-shaped calyx hangs on the stems for some time as the four little seeds develop in each. Blooms from June into September in damp woods, thickets, and meadows over most of the country from Quebec to British Columbia, south to Florida and California.

FIGWORT FAMILY
Scrophulariaceae

Snapdragon, Monkey Flower, Paintbrush, and Penstemon are all members of this very colorful family. The five united petals (rarely four) form an irregular corolla, usually definitely two-lipped and modified for insect attraction and pollination. Often the flowers have dots or lead lines for the bees, and most of them produce nectar. The lower lip is a "landing platform" for insects. The calyx is five-lobed, sometimes irregularly. The flowers are complete, usually with four stamens. A fifth stamen is present in the Penstemons, hence the name, but it has no anther. Mullein is the only Figwort that has five stamens all with anthers (see pg 000). The stamens are attached to the throat of the corolla in pairs. The superior ovary is two-celled, never four-divided on the outside as in the somewhat similar Mints, and forms a many-seeded capsule.

Blue-eyed Mary, *Collinsia verna,* is very much like the western *Collinsia* called Chinese Houses, except *C. verna* has definitely bi-colored blue flowers (upper lobes white, lower bright blue). The *Collinsias* always have the middle lobe of the lower lip folded lengthwise and then often hidden behind the two side lobes. In that fold are the four stamens and the style. The flowers grow in whorls in several spaced tiers up the stem. Each flower is about 2 cm long (.75 in). The opposite leaves

BLUE-EYED MARY

have toothed margins. The stems are slender and usually about 30 cm (12 in) tall. They can be found in moist woods from New York to Wisconsin, south to Iowa, Kansas, and West Virginia. *C. violacea* is very similar but the lower lip is violet and is found from Illinois to Kansas and Texas.

Turtlehead, *Chelone glabra, C. obliqua, C. lyoni,* are tall, stout plants with flowers shaped very much alike. *C. glabra* is usually white with pinkish, yellowish, or purplish lips, *C. obliqua* has pink flowers, and *C. lyoni* is deep pink or crimson. All are shaped somewhat like a turtle's head, with the broad upper lip hovering over the lower lip and nearly hiding it. The stamens are dark and woolly. The flowers are 2-3.5 cm (1-1.5 in) long, crowded together in a terminal spike. The opposite leaves are smooth, bright green and toothed. *C. glabra* and *C. obliqua* have fairly narrow leaves. Turtleheads grow in swamps and along streams throughout much of the east, and west to Kansas and Texas.

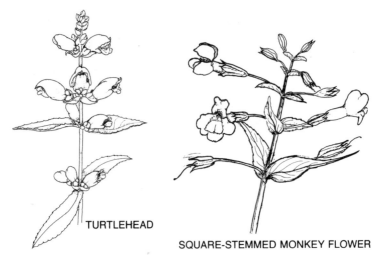

TURTLEHEAD

SQUARE-STEMMED MONKEY FLOWER

Square-stemmed Monkey Flower, *Mimulus ringens,* could be mistaken for a member of the Mint Family because it has a square stem, but it lacks the characteristic odor and hairy leaves and stems; also the ovary is not four-lobed. The flowers are lavender color, two-lipped with a tube about 2.5 cm (1 in) long. The throat of the flowers is nearly closed by a two-ridged yellow palate. The flowers grow on long stalks in pairs from the leaf axils. The opposite, nearly sessile leaves are long-pointed with toothed margins, growing on slender stems. This lavender Monkey Flower grows from 30-60 cm (1-2 ft) tall in damp areas, along streams and swamps practically throughout the east.

PENSTEMON, Beard Tongue. There are many lovely Penstemons in the east, though they are more numerous in the west; they are native Americans. A common name, Beard Tongue, comes from the very hairy fifth stamen, but it is sterile. Penstemons always have five stamens, but four stamens is more characteristic of the Figwort Family. The united petals form a long tube, spreading at the end into two lips—upper lip with two lobes, three in the lower lip. Leaves are always opposite, with upper ones sessile or clasping.

Hairy Beard Tongue, *Penstemon hirsutus,* has several slender hairy stems 20-90 cm (8-36 in) tall, the opposite, clasping leaves very narrow. Even the flowers are soft-hairy, growing in loose clusters. The throat is very hairy, the fifth stamen hairy for half its length. This Penstemon grows from southern Canada through Minnesota and New England to Florida, Alabama, and Missouri, often in dry locations.

HAIRY BEARD TONGUE

Large-flowered Penstemon, *Penstemon grandiflorus,* is a gorgeous, large-flowered species. It may grow more than a meter (3+ ft) tall with large lavender flowers (4-5 cm, 1.5-2 in) long. They are arranged in whorls from axils of clasping, quite round, opposite leaves. The whole plant is beautiful with its smooth, waxy, bluish-green leaves and stems. It is mainly a prairie species from Wisconsin west to Wyoming, south to Illinois and Texas.

Foxglove Penstemon, *Penstemon digitalis,* is the most common white (or whitish) species. It often grows more than a meter tall (3+ ft) in open woods and fields from Maine to South Dakota, south to Virginia, Alabama and Texas. The flowers are 2.5-3 cm long (1+ in), usually with purple lines inside the wide-open, two-lipped corolla. The leaves are clasping, often bronzish, and are sharp-pointed.

Butter-and-eggs or Toadflax, *Linaria vulgaris,* is a common plant all over America, flowering from May to October. They grow 20-90 cm (8-36 in) tall on slender stems with many narrow leaves. The flowers are in a dense terminal cluster of yellow and orange color, shaped much like tiny garden Snapdragons. The corolla of each flower is about 2 cm (.75 in) long, with a spur at its base. The tube and lips are yellow, with an orange palate which nearly closes the tube. It may become a bad weed in gardens, for it spreads underground.

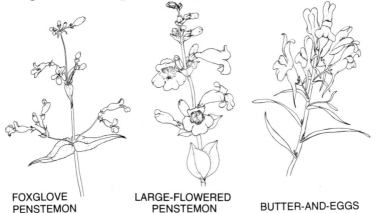

FOXGLOVE
PENSTEMON

LARGE-FLOWERED
PENSTEMON

BUTTER-AND-EGGS

Old-field Toadflax, *Linaria canadensis,* is a common lovely blue
species with larger flowers in sparse spikes, and with a very
slender spur. The palate at the mouth of the tube is white. It
may grow to almost a meter in height, often taking over old
fields (hence common name), especially in sandy areas.

OLD-FIELD TOADFLAX   DOWNY FALSE FOXGLOVE

FALSE FOXGLOVE. There are many False Foxgloves
which, unlike most Figworts, are only slightly two-lipped,
having almost bell-like tips to the tubular flowers. Different
botanists give different names to this group. Some group all
under the genus *Gerardia,* others divide into two genera:
Agalinis, with slender, branching plants and pink or purple
flaring-bell flowers; and *Aureolaria,* with stoutish plants
and bright yellow flaring-bell flowers.

Downy False Foxglove, *Aureolaria (Gerardia) virginica,* has
large showy flowers of clear yellow, the stout plants growing
one to almost two meters tall (3-6 ft). It is a downy plant with
the lower leaves large and deeply lobed, growing oppositely. It
grows in woods from New England west to Michigan, then
south to Florida and Louisiana. Smooth False Foxglove, *Aureolaria (Gerardia) laevigata,* has similar flowers but the leaves
are not lobed or if so, not deeply, and has shorter petioles. The
Fern-leaved False Foxglove, *Aureolaria (Gerardia)
pedicularia,* has fern-like, very finely-divided leaves, the flower
somewhat smaller, and grows mainly in the mountains.

PAINTED-CUP

Painted-cup or Indian Paintbrush, *Castilleja coccinea,* grows from New England to Florida, west to Texas, but the east does not have the variety nor the great masses of Paintbrush that are seen in the west. In Paintbrushes, the flower spike is crowded, the small flowers surrounded by bracts; they and the vividly colored sepals are the most conspicuous part of the flower head. They almost entirely hide the tiny flowers. The corolla is very small with a long, narrow upper lip which encloses the style and four unequal length stamens. The lower lip is very short with three tiny teeth. In *Castilleja coccinea* the scarlet-tipped cylindrical calyx practically encloses the tiny tubular corolla, only the style extending beyond. Then the three-lobed crimson bracts extend often beyond the calyx, giving most of the color to the spike. The leaves are also deeply cleft—usually in threes, the lobes narrow. Plants grow 20-60 cm (8-24 in) high, blooming from April to August in meadows from Maine to Virginia, west to Kentucky, Kansas, and Texas.

HONEYSUCKLE FAMILY
Caprifoliaceae

Most Honeysuckles are shrubs or vines, but since the vines seem to be growing everywhere along fences and roads of the east, their flowers are important to identify. Honeysuckles have a small, five-toothed calyx, five united petals not alike, five stamens which are longer than the corolla, and a three-part, inferior ovary. The style is either lacking or so short it is not noticeable, so the three stigmas are right on top of the ovary itself. The fruit is a several-seeded berry.

Trumpet or Coral Honeysuckle, *Lonicera sempervirens,* has beautiful bright scarlet flowers (or yellow on outside, scarlet inside), with a very long tube—5 cm (2 in). The five rounded lobes on the corolla are only slightly two-lipped; the middle lobe is somewhat larger. The flowers are in scattered whorls along the stem. The large, deep green oval leaves grow oppositely on the somewhat woody vine. On the upper part of the vine, they are roundish and united around the stem. It grows in woods from New England to Florida (it is evergreen in the south), west to Nebraska, flowering March to July.

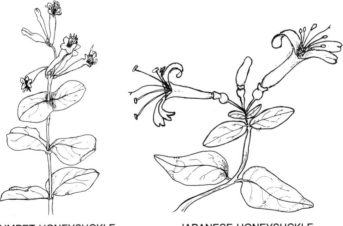

TRUMPET HONEYSUCKLE   JAPANESE HONEYSUCKLE

Japanese Honeysuckle, *Lonicera japonica,* seems to be everywhere in the east, growing as a weedy vine over fences, bushes, and banks for miles. Its creamy blossoms with long, curving stamens have a heavy fragrance. The corolla is much more two-lipped than the Coral Honeysuckle. The evergreen leaves are opposite, the fragrant flowers in their axils. The berry is black. Abundant from Pennsylvania to Georgia, and west to Kansas.

Chapter XI

FLOWERS WITH MORE THAN FIVE PETALS

Thousands of flowers in the world seem to have more than five petals. However, only a few really have more than five *true* petals. Most "many-petaled" flowers will be Composites, like daisies, which are described in the next chapter. Some will be Lilies, Iris, Orchids and others which seem to have six petals, and were described in Chapter IV.

The majority of flowers which *seem* to have six petals really have three sepals and three petals. The sepals and petals are often colored somewhat alike, but actually are arranged in an outer and an inner circle. The three in the outer circle really are sepals and enclose the three in the inner circle, which are the petals. This can be seen especially in the bud stage. When you examine the open flower, you can see how the segments in the outer circle overlap those of the inner circle. These flowers belong to the Lily, Amaryllis, Iris, Orchid, and Spiderwort Families, are built on the plan of three, and have parallel-veined leaves.

The Barberry Family characteristically has more than five true petals and there are two or three other families in the east which have some flowers with more than five true petals. Some members of the Poppy Family may have six or more petals; usually the number of petals is twice the number of sepals though this is not always true. But the many stamens and the type of pistil follow the characteristic

Poppy Family pattern. The common, dainty Star Flower (*Trientalis borealis*) often has seven petals, but the Primrose Family characteristic of each stamen standing in front of (rather than alternating with) each petal is present. Many Water Lilies have more than five petals, but the aquatic plants are covered separately in Chapter XIII.

This chapter includes several flowers which typically have more than five true petals.

POPPY FAMILY

(see characteristics, Chapter V)

Bloodroot, *Sanguinaria canadensis,* is a common early spring flower from Canada to Florida and westward to Texas. It grows 15-30 cm (6-12 in) high on damp slopes, in woods, and along streams, often covering large areas. There is a single, showy, white or pale pinkish flower about 3 cm (1.5 in) across, growing on a leafless orange stem. There are two (or more) sepals which fall as the flower opens. The number of petals varies, but generally there are eight, of two different sizes. There are many stamens with orange anthers and a single pistil which develops into a pod. The name Bloodroot comes from what is really an underground stem. The Indians used it for dye; a broken stem also produces reddish juice. In the spring the first leaf comes up wrapped around the flower stalk. When the flower fades, the bluish-green basal leaf grows larger and the petiole lengthens. The leaf may be 20 cm (8 in) across, palmately lobed and with prominent palmate veining.

Yellow Prickly-Poppy, *Argemone mexicana,* sometimes is called Yellow Thistle because it is a very prickly plant. It grows in sandy roadsides and waste places in the southeast—Florida to Texas and north to Tennessee and Virginia. In the northeast it has escaped from cultivation. The flowers, generally 5 cm (2 in) or more across, usually have six large papery yellow petals, the three sepals falling as the flower opens (sometimes two sepals and four petals). The many stamens also are yellow. The light green leaves have a whitish bloom and are very prickly, appearing thistle-like with prickles even on the veins. They clasp the prickly stem. The compound ovary in the center has reddish stigmas and develops into a very prickly capsule 2 cm or more long. The White Prickly-Poppy or Carolina-Poppy, *Argemone albiflora,* is very similar but has white petals and fewer spines, especially on the veins. The White Prickly Poppy is found along roads from Texas and Florida, north to North Carolina and Missouri.

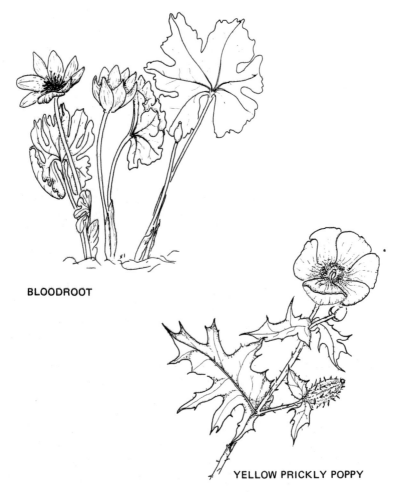

BLOODROOT

YELLOW PRICKLY POPPY

PRIMROSE FAMILY

(see Chapter VII for characteristics)

Star-flower, *Trientalis borealis,* is a dainty, fragile little plant of the woods. The flowers are white and have about seven pointed segments, but the number varies. There is one stamen in front of each petal, whatever the number. Two or three little star-like

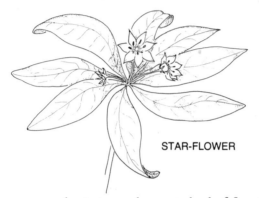

STAR-FLOWER

flowers are on short stems above a whorl of five to ten lance-like leaves up to 13 cm (5 in) long—the flowers about 2 cm across. Grows in cool woods and mountains, Canada to Virginia, flowering from May to August.

BARBERRY FAMILY
Berberidaceae

This is a small family, most of them growing north of the equator, many of them as shrubs. Usually the flowers have four to six sepals, six to eight petals, many stamens (usually about sixteen), and one pistil.

May-Apple, *Podophyllum peltatum,* grows in great masses in practically every woods of the northeast and into the midwest. It is a plant from 25-40 cm tall (10-16 in), the flowering stem with two big, palmately divided and veined, umbrella-like

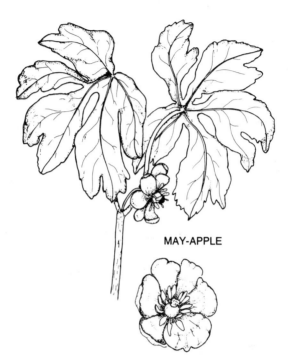

MAY-APPLE

leaves, each 20-24 cm (8-9 in) across—all on a single stalk. The blossom will not be noticed at first, for it grows at the junction of the two leaves and hangs down under them, so frequently one must lift the leaves to see the flowers. The flowers have six to nine white petals, curving slightly inward. There are twice as many stamens and a compound pistil with no style, the large stigmas sitting atop the round ovary. The ovary develops into an "apple," a small green or yellow edible berry. The rest of the plant is said to be *poisonous*. The flowers are beautiful and waxy, about 2.5 cm (1 in) across, but since they hide below the large, conspicuous leaves, they must be searched for. The plants grow on a creeping stem below the ground in woods, hilly areas, and open places over much of the east from Canada to Florida, and westward into Texas and Minnesota, often covering acres with their showy leaves.

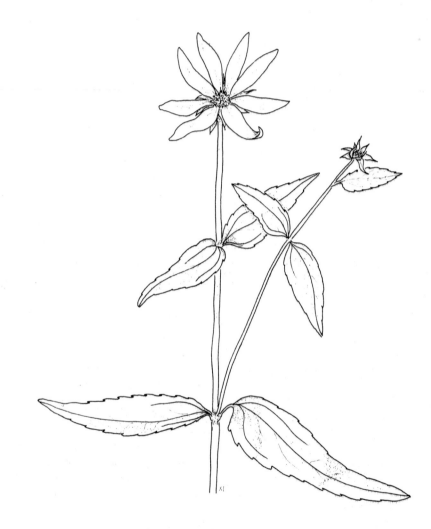

Chapter XII

FLOWERS THAT *SEEM* TO HAVE MANY PETALS

These flowers seem to have many petals, but are not included in Chapter X because only flowers with many *true* petals are included there. Flowers in this chapter are Composite, or compounded of many distinct flowers grouped tightly together at the end of the stems, so that all together they seem to be one big blossom. It is very important to examine them carefully to see the separate flowers. Once you learn the characteristics, it is easy to recognize them as a distinct group, even though there is much variety.

COMPOSITE or SUNFLOWER FAMILY
Compositae

This is the largest flower family, with 10,000 species, found all over the world; about 700 species are recognized in the east. The flowers are extremely specialized for the job of producing seeds. The "flower" is not a single flower, but a collection of flowers in a tight head on a large receptacle, surrounded by an involucre. A spike of flowers, with all the flowers pushed to the top, surrounded by the stem leaves also pushed up, would be similar to a Composite. Each part of the head is typically a tiny complete flower with a calyx, a five-tooth corolla with five attached stamens and a two-parted style. The calyx is modified into a papery or hairy calyx called a pappus, which often stays attached to the seed and helps in distribution, as does the down of a thistle.

Each "petal" really is a single flower, called the "ray flower." These are specialized to advertise and attract pollinating insects. The corolla is often large and becomes one-sided so that, along with the many other ray flowers, it makes a circle of color around the center. The ray flowers may have just stamens or just pistils, or sometimes neither. The "center" of the flower may be made up of many tiny "disc flowers." The corolla of these disc flowers is small and inconspicuous, but a magnifying glass shows it is tubular, flaring slightly into a five-toothed upper edge. The five stamens form a tight collar around the 2-parted style and they typically produce much pollen. Each flower has a one-celled inferior ovary. Sunflower "seeds" are examples of these simple ovaries, the center of the sunflower being a tightly packed collection of dozens of separate disc flowers. The disc flowers are the main seed producers. Gaillardies are excellent flowers to show the general characteristics of this family.

The Sunflower Family is divided into twelve tribes to help make identification easier. We will not give details of the tribes, but since there are three types of flower heads, we will group them this way:

 I. Daisy-like flowers with both ray and disc flowers.
 II. Thistle-like flowers with only disc flowers—the lobes of the tubular corolla often long. The involucral bracts may be spiny.
 III. Dandelion-like flowers with only ray flowers. They typically open out into a large seed head when the tiny flowers mature.

Daisy-like Flowers: Both Ray and Disc Flowers

SUNFLOWERS. There are many sunflowers that are native to America. Indians used their seeds for food, and they are a popular snack food today. The flower heads of the cultivated species grow 30 cm (12 in) or more across, but most of the wild species have heads only several centimeters across. There are twenty to twenty-five species in the east—all are enough alike to be recognized as sunflowers. Only a specialist could expect to know all of them and only a few are included here. The rays are bright yellow, the disc flowers yellowish, brownish, or purplish. The pappus is usually a pair of bristles, and a thin bract, called chaff, is beside each disc flower. The involucre is made of many overlapping green bracts. Plants are often hairy.

Common Sunflower, *Helianthus annuus*, is the state flower of Kansas. It is abundant in the prairies and the west, but also very common along roads in the east, and often grown in gardens. The whole plant is rough with bristly hairs. The disc flowers are dark, the numerous wide ray flowers bright, clear yellow. Each flower head is 7.5-12.5 cm (3-5 in) across, growing alone on the end of a branching stem. The plant may grow to be a meter or so tall, the leaves have three conspicuous veins from the base of the blade.

COMMON SUNFLOWER

Wood Sunflower, *Helianthus strumosus*, has a compact mass of light brown disc flowers, about 2 cm wide, the flowers with chaff mixed in. There are eight to thirteen quite narrow, pointed bright yellow ray flowers. The plant may be as tall as two meters (6 ft), with the toothed leaves generally in pairs, rough above and pale beneath. The stems are generally quite smooth, with a whitish bloom. This sunflower grows from New England west to North Dakota and south to Florida and Texas in dry woodlands.

Swamp Sunflower, *Helianthus angustifolius*, has dark purplish disc flowers in the center of a yellow head about 7.5 cm (3 in) across. The ray flowers are sparse, with only ten or so in each head. The rough, stiff leaves are very narrow, the lower ones may be 12-15 cm (5-6 in) long, growing alternately up the rough stem. These plants grow one to two meters tall (3-6 ft) in swamps and wet places from New York to Florida, west to Kentucky, Missouri, and Texas.

Sneezeweed, *Helenium autumnale*, has bright yellow, turned-back ray flowers with three lobes or notches at the tip of each. These surround a spherical, ball-like, dark yellow center of tiny disc flowers. The 2-5 cm (1-2 in) heads grow on long stems. The plants have stout branching stems with narrow leaves 4-13 cm (2-5 in) long, which grow so close to the stem they seem to cling to it. As one common name (False Swamp Sunflower) indicates, this plant grows in swamps and along streams from Canada to Florida, flowering in early autumn.

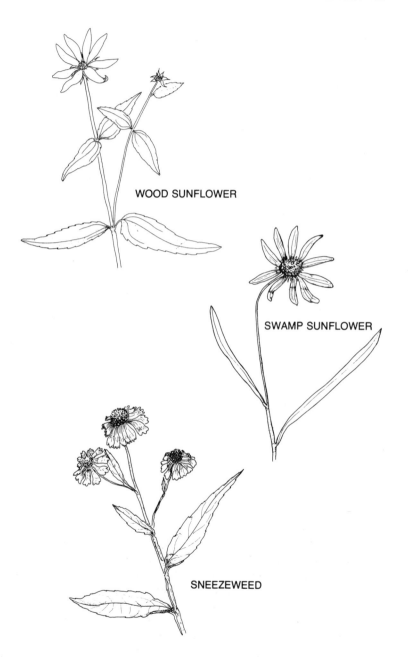

WOOD SUNFLOWER

SWAMP SUNFLOWER

SNEEZEWEED

FLEABANE. There are several Fleabanes, all very much alike, the flowers growing on a flat disc without chaff. All have many, many narrow ray flowers with pistils. The ray flowers may be white, blue or purple, or more rarely, pink. The bracts are reddish, and rather widely but regularly spaced.

Common or Philadelphia Fleabane, *Erigeron philadelphicus*, has flower heads 1-2.5 cm (.5-1 in) across, growing in a panicle. The thick center of tiny yellow disc flowers is surrounded by very numerous (100-150), slender, light pinkish-lavender ray flowers. The slender, softly hairy plants grow 15-75 cm (6-30 in) tall, the leaves clasping the hairy stem. This abundant Fleabane grows in fields and roadsides throughout the United States and most of Canada, usually in damp spots, flowering from April to July or later.

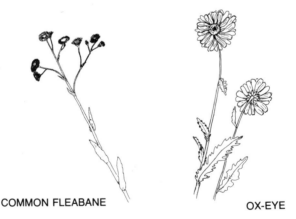

COMMON FLEABANE   OX-EYE

Ox-eye, Marguerite, Common White Daisy, *Chrysanthemum leucanthemum*, is an escaped European flower found all over the United States in fields and along roads—familiar to most Americans. The yellow disc flowers are crowded closely together, with the center sunken. There are twenty or more pure white ray flowers. The heads are 2.5-5 cm (1-2 in) across at tips of branches or of unbranched stems. The leaves are narrow but deeply lobed. Plants grow 60-90 cm (2-3 ft) tall.

COREOPSIS or Tickseeds are common Composites, all very much alike. Usually they have about eight broad yellow ray flowers noticeably 3- or 4-notched or toothed, and seem to be grooved or somewhat folded. The disc flowers are tightly packed on the flat receptacle. The involucre is double—with the lower or outer row of bracts holding the cup-like upper group. The leaves are divided into narrow lobes, the long, naked branches producing a single flower at the tip.

Coreopsis, Lance-leaved Tickseed, *Coreopsis lanceolata*, is the common Coreopsis. The 5 cm (2 in) flower heads are at the tips of slender, naked branches, usually with eight notched rays. The lance-shaped leaves are sessile, often in pairs about half way up the stem, but most of the leaves are low on the plant. They are deeply divided into lance-like lobes. This perennial plant grows from Virginia to Florida, westward to New Mexico, flowering from May through July.

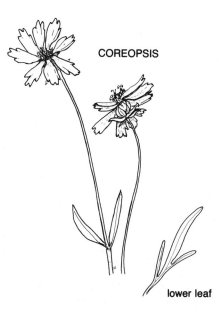

COREOPSIS

lower leaf

Common Tickseed, *Coreopsis major*, grows in the southeastern part of the United States from Virginia to Florida, west to Mississippi, and less commonly north into the midwest. It may be a low plant or grow to almost a meter tall with slender stems and branches. The flower heads usually have eight bright yellow ray flowers, sometimes as much as 2-3 cm (1 in) long, making a showy head. The leaves are paired. They are palmately compound, divided into three very narrow segments. This species is more leafy than most *Coreopsis*.

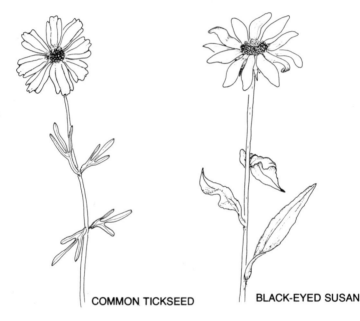

COMMON TICKSEED   BLACK-EYED SUSAN

Black-eyed Susan, *Rudbeckia hirta, R. serotina,* and *R. subtomentosa*, are well-known wildflowers, all very much alike. The showy flower heads are 5-7.5 cm (2-3 in) across. The somewhat cone-shaped disc is dark brown and the ten to twenty long ray flowers are bright yellow. *R. hirta* has very rough and hairy stems and leaves, the lower leaves coarsely toothed. *R. serotina* is not quite so hairy, the leaves quite narrow and not toothed. *R. subtomentosa* has downy stems and deeply cleft leaves. All grow throughout the east and into the midwest, flowering from June into the fall.

Green-headed Coneflower, Tall Coneflower, *Rudbeckia laciniata,* has flower heads 5-7.5 cm (2-3 in) across, with six to ten yellow, drooping ray flowers surrounding the humped greenish-yellow disc flowers. This "cone" becomes very long (tall) after blooming, as the fruits ripen. The plant grows very tall, sometimes as much as 3-4 meters (9-12 ft), the stems with many thin leaves. The basal leaves are deeply pinnately divided into three or five toothed lobes, those on the upper stems are less divided. This plant can be found from Canada to Florida, west to Colorado, flowering in summer in moist, rich spots.

GREEN-HEADED CONEFLOWER   PURPLE CONEFLOWER

Purple Coneflower, *Echinacea purpurea*, has reddish-purple disc and ray flowers, the thirteen to eighteen rays somewhat drooping. The cone is more dome-shaped and not quite as elongated as in the Green-headed Coneflower. The chaff with the disc flowers has long sharp tips, making the center look bristly— which separates this genus from the *Rudbeckias*. The plants have few or no branches, each stem having a single flower head. The tapering leaves (mostly near plant base) have toothed margins and long petioles. Purple Coneflower is found from Virginia to Louisiana and into the midwest.

Mayweed, Dog-fennel, *Anthemis cotula*, has a compact mass of
yellow disc flowers surrounded by ten to twenty white ray
flowers. The center has chaff mixed with the disc flowers. The
leaves are very finely divided, almost fern-like, and have a
disagreeable odor and acrid taste. Some people are allergic to
handling this weed. It is common along roadsides and in fields
all over the United States, flowering all summer.

GOLDEN RAGWORT

MAYWEED

Golden Ragwort, Swamp Squaw-weed, *Senecio aureus*, has
golden yellow ray and disc flowers, with the heads growing in
an open cluster. The flower heads look somewhat "ragged"
because there are only a few rays and they twist and turn. The
involucre is a deep cup-shape. The long-stemmed basal leaves
are heart-shaped, but the stem leaves are long, narrow, and
deeply lobed. Golden Ragwort blooms in the spring in swamps
and wet woods from Canada to Georgia.

Yarrow, Milfoil, *Achillea millefolium*, is a common European weed now all over America. (A native Yarrow, *Achillea lanulosa*, is so similar that it can not be distinguished in the field.) The tiny flower heads grow in flat-topped clusters on stiff, many stemmed plants. Generally there are only five white ray flowers; the very tiny disc flowers are yellow. These perennial plants have such finely divided leaves that they appear fern-like; they are alternate, hairy, and slightly sticky. The plants are 30-90 cm (1-3 ft) tall, blooming from June to September. There are many garden species.

YARROW

ASTER GRANDIFLORUS

ASTERS are familiar wildflowers all over America. There are many species in the east, all much alike. They have involucres composed of rows of overlapping bracts. There are numerous blue, lavender, purple, pink, or occasionally white ray flowers. The disc is usually small, the disc flowers golden yellow, sometimes turning reddish. The leaves are alternate and simple, the plant much branched.

Aster grandiflorus, is a southeastern showy species with flower heads about 5 cm (2 in) across at the ends of long branches with only tiny leaves. The stems and leaves are hairy, the lower leaves up to 7.5 cm (3 in) long and rough. The bract tips of the involucre bend out and then down, especially noticeable on the buds. This aster grows in open woods and fields from Virginia to Florida.

GOLDENRODS are familiar to most Americans. They are native to North America, with about seventy different species in the east, all enough alike to be recognized as Goldenrods, but often hard to tell apart. They are upright plants with very numerous minute heads of flowers containing both ray and disc flowers growing in golden sprays. Usually there are less than ten tiny ray flowers around the small disc flowers. The sprays are made of many slender branches carrying dozens of small heads of flowers. The flower heads may be arranged in slender arching sprays, graceful heavier sprays, slender straight sprays, flat-topped sprays or wide straight sprays. We include only two here. In most species the plants are unbranched, very leafy-stemmed and from 30-120 cm (1-4 ft) tall. Leaves are alternate and usually lance-shaped and toothed.

Canada Goldenrod, *Solidago canadensis*, has such very tiny flower heads that they seem to make a mass of tiny "petals," with so many ray flowers so close together. The disc flowers can be seen only upon close inspection. The flowers grow in a one-sided raceme, forming an arching display. This Goldenrod can be found from Canada and New England to the Carolinas.

Seaside Goldenrod, *Solidago sempervirens*, may grow from almost a meter to two meters tall (2-6 ft) along the Atlantic coast from New England to New Jersey, flowering from July to November. Their flower heads are larger than most Goldenrods, each about .5 cm (.25 in) across. The spray is a straight, fairly wide raceme. The leaves are thick and fleshy, with many along the stem.

CANADA GOLDENROD

SEASIDE GOLDENROD

Thistle-like: Disc Flowers Only

The most familiar members of this group of Composites are the common thistles. Some species are very lovely, most of them showy, but many are considered real pests because they become terrible weeds. They are prolific in their seed production, the seeds carried readily by wind or animals, and some species spread by underground roots. The prickles on leaves and involucres give them the common name of Knight-in-Armor. Thistles have flower heads made up only of tube-shaped disc flowers, the lobes of the corollas unusually long and slender. All thistles have small "seeds" which are carried in the wind by their hairy tip of fluff, or by hooks which catch in fur and are carried by animals. The thistle is the national emblem of Scotland. Some garden flowers that belong in the thistle group are Bachelor's Button and Corn Flower. Young, peeled flower stems can be eaten like celery. The down of the seed is useful for fire tinder.

Canada Thistle, *Cirsium arvense*. This small lavender thistle is a common weed of the north, especially in Canada, but also throughout much of the United States. It has small heads of lavender disc flowers about 2.5 cm (1 in) across. The involucre is urn-shaped and not as prickly as most thistles. The leaves are 5-10 cm wide (2-4 in). They and the stems are quite spiny. The plant grows 30-150 cm tall (1-5 ft) in dense patches along roadsides and in fields. It spreads not only by its abundant seeds but by deep underground rootstocks. It resembles Knapweed (*Centaurea maculosa*) until you look closely, especially at the leaves.

Bull Thistle, *Cirsium vulgare*, is a common purple biennial thistle, introduced from Eurasia and now established over most of North America. It grows 60-150 cm tall (2-5 ft) with many spiny branches. The involucre is very prickly and is very noticeable since it is vase-shaped and not surrounded by leaves. The leaves are deeply cut and spiny-edged—the spines yellowish.

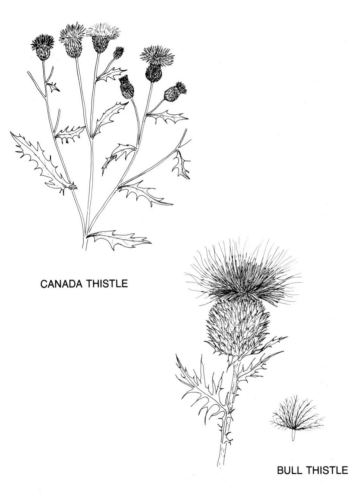

CANADA THISTLE

BULL THISTLE

The upper side is covered with stiff hairs and a spiny ridge runs from the base of each leaf, along the stem, to the next leaf—a distinguishing characteristic. The "seeds" are wind-carried by their thistledown, and each has a spongy ring that breaks and releases the seed when it absorbs water. It likes fairly moist areas in fields and along roads, low elevations to mountains all over the country, blooming from late June to September—a terrible weed.

Swamp Thistle, *Cirsium muticum*, grows one to almost three meters tall (3-8 ft), with slender, branching stems. The heads of the flowers are about 3 cm (1.5 in) across, with rose-purple disc flowers enclosed in a round involucre of closely lapped bracts which have no prickles, but are sticky and cobwebby. The leaves are deeply divided and somewhat hairy, forming a long-stemmed basal rosette. The upper leaves are sessile and less divided. This is a common plant in swamps and moist fields from Canada to Florida, west to Texas, flowering all summer.

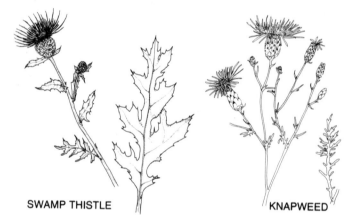

SWAMP THISTLE   KNAPWEED

Knapweed, *Centaurea maculosa*. Whole fields of this late-summer, early-fall wildflower can be found. Your first thought is that the field or roadside is a mass of lavender asters, but when looked at closely, you realize it is not an aster, since there aren't both ray and disc flowers.

The plant is many-branched, 30-90 cm (1-3 ft) high, with the lower leaves considerably larger than the upper ones. All the leaves show such deep divisions that at first glance you think they are simple, very narrow leaves—they are not at all prickly. Many flowers are on each branch, blooming from the tip first. They are a clear lavender-pink, with the head held at the base by a vase-shaped collection of bracts. Each bract has a black tip, giving the involucre a spotted appearance. The tiny flowers are numerous, twenty-five to fifty per head. The pollen matures early, then the long slender pistil grows out beyond the circle of stamens.

Barnaby's Thistle, Yellow Star Thistle, *Centaurea solstitialis*, is a small, bright yellow, prickly, branching annual thistle found along roads, wild areas, and fields over much of the east. The brilliant shiny yellow corollas of the tiny disc flowers are tubular and divided into long lobes. The involucral bracts surrounding the round flower heads have prickles 1.5-2 cm long (½-¾ in) long, and the upper bracts are winged. These shiny bracts help give it the name Yellow Star Thistle. The shiny wings become hard, the prickles persist, and the plant dries to form a whitish prickly tangle which becomes a great nuisance. It grows 30-45 cm (12-18 in) tall with small leaves along its stiff slender branches. The leaves are not spiny-edged in this group of thistles, but are attached by their midrib along the stem for part of their length, giving the stem a winged or angled appearance. The basal leaves are divided, leaves and stems covered with gray cottony hairs. This terrible weed, especially in grain fields, was introduced from Europe and is spreading and ruining much valuable agricultural and grazing land. It begins to bloom near the time of the summer solstice, which gives it the species name.

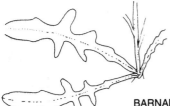

BARNABY'S THISTLE

Sweet Joe-Pye Weed, *Eupatorium purpureum*, has a mass of pale pinkish, whitish, or purplish flower heads clustered in a broad, somewhat bristly, fuzzy inflorescense. Each flower head has about ten to twelve tiny disc flowers. Joe-Pye Weed is common in damp areas from New England to Florida, to Oklahoma, the stout, tall plants to two meters (6 ft). The pointed leaves are sharply toothed and grow in whorls of three to six (most often four) around the stem. They may smell like vanilla when crushed. The stem usually has a whitish bloom, and may be purple- or black-spotted at the leaf nodes. Spotted Joe-Pye Weed (*E. maculatum*) is very similar, but the stem is purple-spotted along its length. This plant was named after an Indian, who thought it had medicinal use.

Boneset or Common Thoroughwort, *Eupatorium perfoliatum*, is another of the several Thoroughworts found in the east. All are tall, stout plants topped by a flat, fuzzy cluster of small heads of disc flowers blooming from late summer to fall. The Common Thoroughwort has white flowers and long pointed leaves which are tough, veiny, wrinkled, and hairy, growing united around the stem, at least near the base of the plant. *Eupatorium hyssopifolium* also has white flowers, but it has narrow, little leaves in whorls of three or four thickly scattered up the stem, with small leaf clusters in each axis. The flowers of both are shaped much like the Joe-Pye Weeds and are common in wet meadows from New England to Florida to Louisiana, flowering in late summer.

White Snakeroot, *Eupatorium rugosum*, also has small white flowers much like Boneset, with many heads of disc flowers growing in a loose cluster on a tall plant. However, the oval, thin, sharply toothed leaves of Snakeroot are not sessile or whorled, but are petioled and opposite on the slender stem.

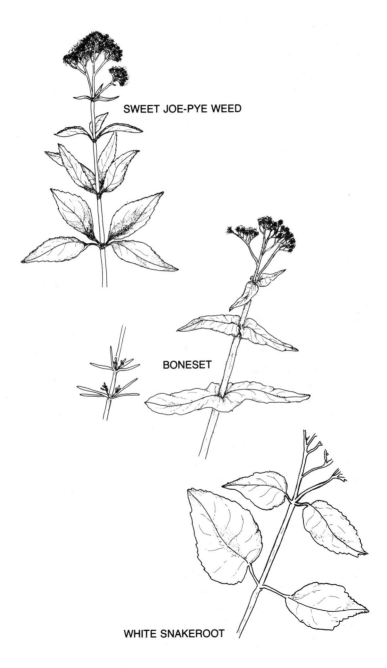

SWEET JOE-PYE WEED

BONESET

WHITE SNAKEROOT

Tansy, *Tanacetum vulgare*, has small flower heads made up of hundreds of tiny disc flowers crowded onto a dome-shaped, or button-like head, which gives an almost smooth appearance because the disc flowers are so tiny and so closely packed together. The plant has a strong spicy odor. The leaves are alternate and are so deeply lobed they appear fernlike. The stems are tall and stiff. This plant becomes a pest in gardens because it increases rapidly. Tansy makes masses of golden color all summer over much of Canada and the United States.

Common Pearly Everlasting, *Anaphalis margaritacea*, is truly a common plant, for it is found over most of the United States. It is unusual because the dozens of round flower heads appear white with small yellow or brown centers. This is because the flowers really are just heads of tiny disc flowers and the many bracts of the bulging involucre are shiny, white, and papery, even in bud. As the flowers mature, they too become white and soft-fuzzy, the bracts spread out and the whole flower stalk dries and is more or less "everlasting."

Ten to fifteen flower heads grow in a cluster, with many such clusters grouped together at the top of each leafy white stem. The alternate leaves are long and narrow, 10 cm (4 in) long at the base to 2.5 (1 in) at the upper ends of the stems. The stems and the leaves—especially the undersides—are very gray and woolly. Many stems grow from a perennial base. If you examine the flower heads with a magnifying glass, you find mostly heads with tiny pistillate flowers with perhaps a few staminate flowers. Other plants will produce only staminate flowers, which of course produce no seeds. The minute corolla of the pistillate flower is thread-like, the style extending beyond it. Everlasting tends to bloom all summer.

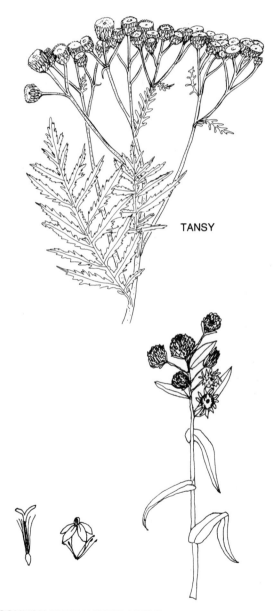

TANSY

COMMON PEARLY EVERLASTING

Ray Flowers Only

This group of Composites have heads with ray flowers only. The member known to almost everyone everywhere is the Dandelion. This group is large, with members all over the world. Most of the plants have milky, bitter juice, and leaves are generally basal. The flower stalks are hollow, usually leafless, with a single head of flowers at the top, or several in a small cluster. The flowers are on a naked flat receptacle, leaving a smooth surface when the seeds have blown away.

Dandelion, *Taraxacum officinale*, is a lawn pest all over the world. The flower heads are bright yellow each morning, but close before night. The bracts then turn up around the withered flower head. The seeds mature very rapidly—so a few days later the bracts open and turn back on the stem and you see the fluffy seed head on its now-elongated stalk. The fluffy white pappus scatters the seeds everywhere, carried by the wind. Young tender leaves of this plant are used for greens, salads, or can be fried. Roots are made into a drug, taraxacum, or can be roasted until dark brown and ground to make a coffee substitute. Dandelions make miles of fields golden with their yellow heads—the common name coming from the French *dent de lion*, referring to the "teeth" on the basal leaves.

DANDELION

Chicory, *Cichorium intybus*, has a deep tap root which can be roasted and ground into a coffee substitute. The flower heads of this plant in some varieties are pink or yellow, but the most common one is a beautiful, unmistakable shade of china blue. The blossoms are dainty and attractive, but the color is the outstanding characteristic. Each ray is five-toothed at the tip and 1-2.5 cm long (.5-1 in). Chicory has large toothed or pinnately cleft basal leaves but the flowering stalks are almost leafless, growing 30-90 cm (12-36 in) tall. Chicory grows throughout the United States and southern Canada, flowering from summer into fall.

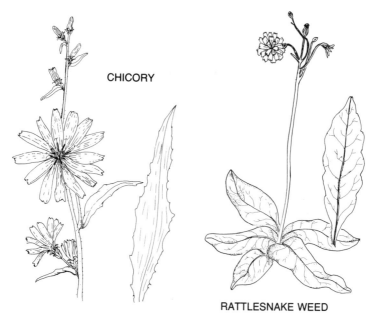

CHICORY

RATTLESNAKE WEED

Rattlesnake-weed, *Hieracium venosum*, has a flower head which resembles a small pale dandelion head but there are several on the slender leafless stem, which is about 60 cm tall (24 in). The common name comes from the marking on the basal leaves—purple veins or splotches. The heads of ray flowers are about 2 cm across (.75 in), each ray flower toothed at the tip. This plant grows in sandy soil from New England west to Michigan, south to Florida and Louisiana, flowering all summer.

Orange Hawkweed, Devil's Paintbrush, *Hieracium auran-tiacum*, has bright orange, flattish, dandelion-like flower heads, but there are several borne on short branches at the top of the 15-48 cm (6-20 in) naked stems. It paints fields and meadows orange all summer from Canada to Virginia. The orange ray flowers are five-toothed at the tip. The stem and the long, smooth-margined leaves of the basal rosette are very hairy.

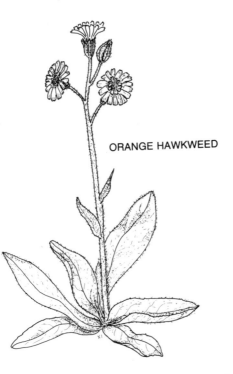

ORANGE HAWKWEED

Oyster-Plant or Salsify, *Tragopogon porrifolius*, is best known by its very large tan or brown seed head 7.5 cm (3 in) or more across. It looks like a huge brown dandelion head, each "seed" having a parachute of fine pappus hairs attached to the achene. The flat, deep purple heads of ray flowers are attractive and showy, growing at the tip of a 30-120 cm (1-4 ft) hollow stem. The outer ray flower corollas are much longer than those toward the center; each is five-toothed at the tip, and has both stamens and pistils. The head is surrounded by long slender

OYSTER PLANT

bracts in one row, extending beyond the rays. These perennial herbs have milky juice, a thick taproot, and long, clasping, grass-like leaves. It was brought to America by the early colonists and has since escaped. The root makes a good vegetable, tasting somewhat like oysters or parsnips—it should be used before the stalk blossoms: scrape, slice, and cook like carrots. This species is cultivated in some areas for its root. The milky juice was coagulated and used by the Indians to chew like gum. The flower opens in the morning, usually closing by noon, and wilting quickly if picked. As the seeds mature, the head reopens as a big fluffy ball. Oyster-Plant grows along moist roadsides over most of the United States, blooming from May to July, with seed heads seen everywhere in the early fall. Yellow Goat's Beard, *Tragopogon major* and *Tragopogon pratensis*, is a common name for two yellow species. *T. major* has flowers with long (5 cm) bracts and the stem is swollen or enlarged under the flower head (as in the purple species). *T. pratensis* has yellow flowers with short bracts (2.5 cm) and the stem is not swollen under the flower head. Both can be found commonly from Canada south to Georgia and Tennessee.

Chapter XIII

AQUATIC PLANTS

One of the most impressive sights in the east to anyone from the drier parts of American is the numerous swamps, ponds, and slow-running streams. Most of such places are filled or bordered with lush plants of several kinds. We have grouped some of them together in this last chapter.

BUTTERCUP FAMILY
Ranunculaceae

(see Chapter III for family characteristics)

White Water Buttercup, Crowfoot, *Ranunculus circinatum (longirostris)*, grows entirely in water, often with Blue Flag. The finely divided leaves (almost hair-like) and stems grow under the water, with only the flowers above the water. The five white petals and five green sepals form a small flower only about 1 cm (½ in) across. These are widespread in ponds and slow streams across Canada and south to North Carolina, Tennessee and Texas, flowering all summer. It is also to be found in Europe and Asia.

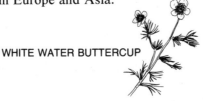

WHITE WATER BUTTERCUP

WATER PLANTAIN FAMILY
Alismaceae

The members of this family are marsh or aquatic herbs with thickened, long, tuberous rootstocks and very long-petioled basal leaves which grow erect above the water. There are three greenish persistent sepals and three white deciduous petals. Usually there are many stamens (though there may be as few as six). There are many one-celled ovaries which develop into achenes. The plants have milky juice.

ARROWHEAD

Arrowhead, Tule Potato, *Sagittaria latifolia,* gets its common name from the shape of its leaves, which can be seen growing above the water in ponds and swamps almost throughout North America. Each leaf is variable in size, but may be 5-30 cm (2-12 in) long, pointed at upper end and with sharp basal lobes. The young leaves have no blades, just petioles. Mature leaves develop the "arrowhead shape." The flowers grow in whorls of three on the upper end of the flowering stalk. Each waxy white flower has three petals which soon drop and three shorter green sepals which persist. There are many stamens, the upper flowers staminate and the lower ones on the stalk usually pistillate. The numerous ovaries are crowded into a dense round head, each developing into a flat, winged achene with the style forming a beak. These plants are so beautiful and interesting they usually are included in any collection for pond gardens. The tubers are edible.

PICKERELWEED FAMILY
Pontederiaceae

There are only about six members of this family in the east, but these are so numerous that they cover acres. They are aquatic plants, either floating on the surface of the water or rooted in muddy banks. The flowering stems are topped with a dense spike or cluster of blue or lilac flowers. The two-lipped flowers are tubular, with six lobes. There are three lobes in the upper lip, with the middle lobe the longest, and three spreading lobes in the lower lip. There are six stamens, three of them longer than the others. The calyx is persistent around the one-seeded fruit. The large, glossy green leaves are arrowhead- or heart-shaped, or round. Some members of the family have splotches of purple on the leaves. Some become serious weeds because they are so rank they fill rivers and lakes until they are choked.

Pickerelweed, *Pontederia cordata,* has lovely spikes of blue flowers growing so densely they color acres of swamps and shallow waters from New England to Florida, west to Minnesota and Texas, flowering from early spring through autumn. There are many flowers in the spike, each flower tubular and about .5 cm long. Each violet-blue flower is marked with a yellow-green spot. The three upper lobes of the corolla are partly united, the lower three lobes spreading. Below the flower spike is a thin, spathe-like bract. The big, glossy, arrowhead-shaped leaves are almost as attractive as the flower spikes.

Water Hyacinth, *Eichornia crassipes,* is another member of this family which has become a serious problem in some areas. It chokes rivers and lakes with its rank growth, and so is a pest, but its flowers are very beautiful. The large rounded leaves float on the water because of the inflated leaf-stalks which have balloon-like, spongy enlargements under the leaves. The flowers are large—blue, purple or nearly white. They are slightly irregular with six lobes to the corolla, the upper lobe marked

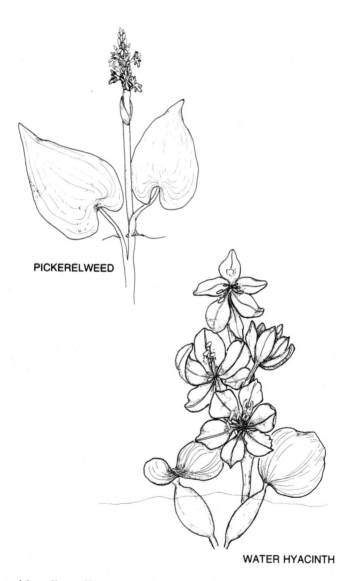

PICKERELWEED

WATER HYACINTH

with yellow. They grow in the southeastern states around the Gulf of Mexico from Texas to Florida, north to Virginia and Missouri. They are tropical plants which have invaded our waters.

WATER LILY FAMILY
Nymphaeaceae

Water Lilies are lush, big-leaved plants growing abundantly in the numerous still waters of the east. They are not true Lilies at all. Some of them are annuals, some are perennial, but they grow from rhizomes which anchor them in the mud. They have big round leaves which float on the surface of the water (or stand above it), and are attached in the center to long stems which extend down to the mud. There are channels in the stems which are filled with a gas that circulates through them. The solitary flowers have three to six sepals, many petals and many stamens. The outer stamens tend to become progressively petal-like. The pistil is large and many-parted, usually with many stigmas. The flowers often have a heavy fragrance.

Fragrant Water Lily, White Water Lily, *Nymphaea odorata,* is the common white Pond Lily found in quiet waters. The waxy, fragrant white (sometimes pinkish) flowers may be 20 cm (8 in) across, and open mainly in the mornings. There are four green or colored sepals and many petals, the inner rows becoming narrower and narrower. The numerous stamens are brilliant yellow. The many-parted pistil develops into nutlets which Indians used for food. The dark green leaves are oval-round, deeply cleft at the base, purple on the lower side. Fragrant Water Lilies grow from Canada to Florida and on into Mexico and South America.

Common Spatterdock, Yellow Pond Lily, *Nuphar advena,* has leaves which look very much like those of the White Water Lily, though usually they are more oval, and they stand erect above the water rather than floating. The flowers are very different, for they are cup-shaped and much smaller. Also, the many sepals are a noticeable feature—usually there are three greenish ones, then three larger yellowish ones which are quite thick and curl up around the many small, almost scale-like petals, the many stamens, and the large pistil. Yellow Pond

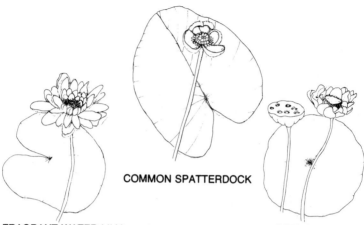

COMMON SPATTERDOCK

FRAGRANT WATER LILY   LOTUS LILY

Lily often fills entire areas with lovely big round leaves. They
grow all through the east. Bullhead Lily, *Nuphar variegatum,*
is very common also and quite similar, but its leaves float on
the water, not stand above it.

Lotus Lily, Water Chinquapin, *Nelumbo lutea,* sometimes is
called "Sacred Bean" because of the unusual seeds which the
Indians prized as food. The tubers are edible also. A large,
flat-topped "cone" structure is in the center of each flower. In
each of its many holes is a pistil, so the seeds are embedded in
it—each seed about 1 cm (.5 in) in diameter. The flowers are
pale yellow and very fragrant. They may be as much as 25 cm
(10 in) across. Their many sepals grade into the numerous petals, both curling up around the large center with its numerous
stamens and many-parted ovary. The leaves of this plant are
one continuous big circle, with no indentations, the stem attached to the slightly depressed center. These leaves usually
grow above the water, not floating on the surface, the blossoms
also stand above the water. It grows all over the east, often
covering entire ponds or river areas from New England to
Florida, west to the Mississippi Valley. Lotus Lily is not as
common as the Fragrant Water Lily or the Yellow Pond Lily,
but very abundant in some areas.

Glossary

Achene: Small, dry, one-seeded fruit that doesn't break open.

Annual: Growing anew from seed each year.

Anther: The part of the stamen that produces the pollen.

Biennial: Not blooming until the second year.

Blade: Flat, expanded part of the leaf (also of a petal if lower end of petal is narrowed into a claw).

Bloom: Of leaves, stem, or fruit—it appears whitened with powder.

Bract: Modified or small-sized leaf of a flower cluster.

Bulb: Cluster of modified fleshy storage leaves underground.

Calyx: Term used when speaking of all the sepals.

Capsule: A dry seed pod which opens in one of several ways.

Claw: The narrowed base of a petal.

Corm: A thickened, underground, solid fleshy stem base, such as a Gladiolus.

Corona: A "crown" of cup-like structures standing above the reflexed petals in milkweeds.

Corolla: Term used when speaking of all the petals.

Epiphyte: Plant growing on a tree (not a parasite).

Filament: Stem supporting the anther in a stamen.

Genus: A plant group made up of different species; the first part of a scientific name; plural: *genera*.

Head: A tight group of flowers.

Herb: A plant without woody parts above ground; annual, biennial, or perennial.

Inflorescence: The flowering part of the plant; the arrangement of individual flowers.

Involucre: A circle of bracts surrounding a cluster of flowers, as at base of umbel in the Parsley Family (*Umbelliferae*), or around the head as in the Sunflowers (Composites).

Lanceolate: Lance-shaped; broader end toward base.

Legume: Seed pod which opens on each side into two parts, as peas.

Node: The place on the stem where a leaf is attached.

Ovary: The base of the pistil, where the seeds develop.

Palate: a projection at the throat of a tubular corolla.

Panicle: A branching flower cluster.

Pappus: The modified calyx of Composites—usually pappery, hairy, scaly, etc.

Peduncle: The stem of a flower or flower cluster.

Perennial: Living more than one year.

Perfect: A flower with both stamens and pistils in same flower.

Petals: The parts of the corolla; the inner circle of the floral envelope, usually colored. If only one circle (as in Anemones), botanists call them sepals.

Petiole: The stalk (stem) of a leaf.

Pistil: The female, or seed-producing part of the flower. Includes the stigma, style and ovary.

Pistillate: Referring to a flower or plant producing only pistils, no stamens.

Pod: Any dry fruit that splits open.

Raceme: Flowers in elongated clusters along a single stalk; youngest flower at top.

Receptacle: Enlarged part of stem where flower parts attach.

Reflexed: Turned downward or backward.

Saccate: Part distended or sack-like.

Saprophyte: Plant living on decaying material; contains no chlorophyll.

Sepals: The parts of the calyx; the outer circle of the floral envelope. Protects flower.

Sessile: Sits on something directly, with no stalk or stem (as a sessile leaf).

Spadix: A thick-stemmed spike of tiny flowers with no petals, usually partially enclosed by a spathe.

Spathe: A large bract enclosing a tight flower cluster.

Spike: Flowers with no stems (peduncles); each flower sessile on stalk.

Spur: A slender and hollow extension of some flower part, as a petal of Columbine.

Stamen: The male or pollen-producing organ; includes anther and filament.

Staminate: Referring to flower or plant with only stamens, no pistils.

Staminoidea: Stamens which produce no pollen.

Stigma: Portion of pistil that receives the pollen.

Stipules: Small appendages in pairs at base of leaf petiole, as in roses.

Tendril: A slender stem portion which helps plants cling.

Umbel: Branches growing from same point, and reaching same height; may refer to flowers, flower clusters, or leaves.

Whorl: Three or more leaves growing from same level on stalk.

Bibliography

Britton, Nathaniel Lord and Addison Brown, *Illustrated Flora of the Northern United States, Canada, and the British Possessions*. Three volumes, paperback. New York: Dover, 1970.

Brown, Clair A., *Wildflowers of Louisiana and Adjoining States*. Baton Rouge: Louisiana State University, 1972.

Dean, Blanche, *Wildflowers of Alabama and Adjoining States*. University of Alabama Press, 1973.

Dormon, Caroline, *Flowers Native to the Deep South*. Harrisburg, PA: J. Horace McFarland Co.

Duncan, W.H. and Leonard Foote, *Wildflowers of the Southeastern United States*. Athens, GA: University of Georgia Press, 1974.

Fernald, Merritt Lyndon, *Gray's Manual of Botany*. 8th ed. New York: Van Nostrand, 1970.

Gilbert, Lydia N., *Wild Flowers and State Flowers of North America*. New York: G. Sully & Co., 1930.

Gray, Asa. *Gray's Manual of Botany, A Handbook of Flowering Plants and Ferns of the Central and Northeastern United States and Adjacent Canada*. Edited by M.L. Fernald. 8th ed. New York: Van Nostrand, Reinhold, 1970.

Greene, Wilhelmina F. and H.L. Blomquist, *Flowers of the South, Native and Exotic*. Chapel Hill: University of North Carolina Press, 1953.

House, Homer D., *Wild Flowers*. New York: Macmillan, 1934.

Hylander, Clarence John, *The Macmillan Wild Flower Book*. New York: Macmillan, 1960.

Kieren, John, *An Introduction to Wild Flowers*. New York: Hanover House, 1952.

Klimas, John Edward, *Wildflowers of Eastern America.* Knopf, 1974.

Lemmon, Robert Stell, *Wildflowers of North America in Full Color.* New York: Hanover House, 1961.

Mathews, F. Schuyler and Norman Taylor, *Field Book of American Wild Flowers.* New York: Putnam, 1955.

Morcombe, M., *Wildflowers of the East Coast.* Mystic, CT: Periwinkle Books, 1974.

————*Wildflowers of the North and Centre.* Mystic, CT: Periwinkle Books, 1974.

Peterson, Roger Tory, *A Field Guide to Wildflowers of Northeastern and North-central North America.* Hoston: Houghton Mifflin Co., 1968.

Rickett, Harold William, *New Field Book of American Wild Flowers.* New York: Putnam, 1963.

————*The Odyssey Book of American Wildflowers.* New York: Odyssey Press, 1964.

————*Wild Flowers of the United States.* Volume 1: *Northeastern States,* Volume 2: *Southeastern States.* New York: McGraw Hill, 1966-1973.

Small, J.K., *Manual of the Southeastern Flora.* New York: Hafner, 1972.

Stupka, Arthur, with the Eastern Park and Monument Association, *Wildflowers in Color.* New York: Harper & Row, 1965.

Walcott, Mary Morris, *Wild Flowers of America.* New York: Crown Publications, 1953.

Watts, May, *Flower Finder: A Manual for Identifying Spring Wildflowers and Flower Families East of the Rockies.* Jackson, Mississippi: Nature Study, 1955.

Zim, Herbert S. *Flowers—a Guide to Familiar American Wildflowers.* New York: Simon & Schuster.